PINO NANO

Natuzza Evolo

- the movie of her life-

-The story of Natuzza Evolo, the Calabrian mystic who claimed she could "talk to the dead, see the Virgin Mary, meet the guardian angel, and talk to Jesus", and who, around the time of Easter, lived the mystery of blood and the stigmata-

Rome 2022

Titles of the same author

Calabritudine
Calabriamerica
Non Solo Mafia
Lorenzo
Il mio Paese
Prima Pagina
Storie di successi
Cara Sant'Onofrio
Calabresi di Chicago
Beyond the wall of silence
Il Romanzo della politica
La TV delle Regioni: Radiotelevisione, memoria di una regione
40 Anni di Rai in Calabria, Prima Parte
40 Anni di Rai in Calabria, Seconda Parte
Giuseppe Borgia, Storia di un Grand Commis di Stato

-(For this work, nothing will ever be due to Pino Nano. Each euro earned will go to the Immaculate Heart of Mary Refuge of Souls Foundation) -

ISBN

Index

-The case of Natuzza Evolo. - A story of great media impact -

1 The life of the Calabrian medium and an extraordinary legend

2 Natuzza's blood: Testimonies from the doctors who treated her

3 Father Agostino Gemelli condemns Natuzza to isolation

4 The witnessed miracles performed by Natuzza in the mental institution

5 Natuzza marries Pasquale Nicolace and gives birth to five children

6 Natuzza Evolo "I am only an earthworm ..."

7 Stigmata and blood sweat, the ordeal of Natuzza Evolo

8 Pino Nano meets Natuzza Evolo for the first (but not the last) time

9 The real miracles performed by Natuzza are those revealed by the people she met

10 Monsignor Domenico Tarcisio Cortese, the priest who changed Natuzza's life

11 Valerio Marinelli, the nuclear engineer who became the official biographer of Natuzza Evolo

13 Sergio Zavoli holds her face in his hands and she reconciles him with God

14 "Natuzza helped me beat cancer", says Ruggero Pegna

15 Mon.Renzo confirms "A new investigation is required. The process of beatification is suspended"

16 Natuzza and her intimate relationship with Jesus

17 "Why the rush to make Natuzza a saint? Her miracles? Many cases of alleged healings."

18 Every day, a thousand fresh flowers on Natuzza's grave

19 Don Attilio Nostro: "Natuzza, prophecy and fulfilment"

20 "The Basilica will be finally consecrated in August 2022"

21 Natuzza Evolo: her first official biography by ICSAIC

22 Notes

PINO NANO

Natuzza Evolo

- the movie of her life-

The story of Natuzza Evolo, the Calabrian mystic who claimed she could "talk to the dead, see the Virgin Mary, meet the guardian angel, and talk to Jesus", and who, around the time of Easter, lived the mystery of blood and the stigmata

As a journalist and editor-in-chief at RAI Calabria, then head of TGR National Agency in Rome, Pino Nano had the privilege of meeting Natuzza Evolo several times. These meetings resulted in some television specials and reports that, over the years, have contributed to introducing this figure to the world. The following is the treatment of a documentary film on this woman who, throughout her life, has enlivened a debate that aroused controversy and reflections in the most accredited scientific fora, and that finally convinced the Vatican to initiate the process of canonization for Natuzza Evolo, which is currently in progress.

The cover photo refers to the special documentary about Natuzza Evolo by Rai Vaticano, "The way of the Cross" (by Pino Nano and Filippo Di Giacomo) that Rai Uno broadcast on Good Friday 6thApril 2012.

The case of Natuzza Evolo
- A story of great media impact -
The life of the Calabrian medium and an extraordinary legend

by Pino Nano

Natuzza Evolo died eleven years ago, on November 1, 2009. Yet, the story of this woman, who "talked to the dead", who could "bilocate", who invoked "miracles", who had stigmata on her hands and feet, who, around the time of Easter experienced the "phenomenon of hemography", who "communicated with the Virgin Mary and could see the Guardian Angel", who "spoke in languages she didn't know", and who could also "see the future", has everything it takes to become the subject of a high-impact film, television series, or play.

To spread her truths, a fully developed, inspiring documentary film in Italian, English, and Spanish, should be distributed all over the world.

If I were a director or producer, I would take the amazing books written in recent years on the subject (these include, among others, *Il Ponte di San Giacomo*, the first essay by Maria Luigi Lombardi Satriani, who has provided a faithful and exhaustive reconstruction of the facts) as a starting point, and I would make it a subject for an Italian television audience.

I would ask Valerio Marinelli, an illustrious physicist and university professor, as well as the author of at least ten different publications, who knows more about Natuzza than her children or grandchildren, to edit the texts. Then, I would ask historian Rocco Turi, who is also a manic sociologist specializing in studies of suburbs, to organize the scenography, in order to reconstruct the places where Natuzza "saw the Virgin Mary" for the first time, and where she lived and spent her extraordinary life.

Finally, I would ask Luigi Maria Lombardi Satriani and Vito Teti – two highly sophisticated ethnologists – for a final draft review, and I would create a two-episode television series, in Italian, Spanish, and English, and I would submit it to the 2021 Venice International Film Festival with full confidence.

Later I would submit it directly to the much larger international movie industry. A well-done job – I am sure – would be much appreciated, as the true story of Natuzza Evolo is fascinating and is unique to television. RAI (Radiotelevisione Italiana) has already shown its interest in the "Natuzza phenomenon", when it offered its audience a series of television specials that produced unexpected ratings in the history of Italian television.

The episode of "Detto tra Noi" – a RAI 2 television show written and presented by Piero Vigorelli – on Natuzza Evolo, aired on December 8, 1994, the feast of the Immaculate Conception in Italy, was watched by over 6 million people. It was early in the afternoon, and it definitely broke a ratings record.

Today, ninety-six years after Natuzza Evolo was born, and twelve years after she has passed, the time has come to focus on this ambitious project. In fact, the Church has already officially initiated the process of beatification of Natuzza, and, sooner or later, once the details on the events that occurred within the Foundation regarding the relationship with the Diocesi di Mileto are finally clarified, we will learn more about the official position of the Holy See.

Fortunately, the Vatican is now seeing the situation with new eyes, compared to the past, also thanks to the extraordinary work carried out, in recent years, by the current Bishop of Mileto, Monsignor Luigi Renzo, a modern and versatile intellectual journalist, who represents a Church that has evolved in recent years and that has learnt how to keep up with the times.

Without a doubt, no one at the top of the Catholic Church's hierarchy seems to question the veracity of the "Natuzza Evolo phenomenon" anymore, nor the "sacred fruits" of her earthly experience. Many say that Natuzza will be proclaimed a saint sooner than expected by the Vatican, but no one knows how or when.

In the impenetrable rooms of the Congregation for the Causes of Saints, where everyone carefully chooses his or her words, the sense is that Natuzza has already become, despite herself, an important witness of Christ and an example of Christian piety in Italy.

It may be provocative to President Jole Santelli, but let the Region make a movie about the life of Natuzza Evolo, perhaps with the support of the Calabria Film Commission. I am formally applying to work on this project for free for the rest of my life.

Believe me, no one could represent our popular piety and Christian tradition in the world better than the "woman who received the stigmata", as today Natuzza is the most authentic symbol of generous faith, and the most recognizable icon of Calabria.

However, such a project – which is definitely brave – could be jeopardized by the inaccuracy and the complexity that characterize regional bureaucracies. As such, this project may never see the light. I've been intrigued with the case of Natuzza Evolo for forty years and desire nothing more than to share her wisdom and journey.

There are bibliographic notes available that could introduce someone to Natuzza's legacy.

Natuzza's blood: Testimonies from the doctors who treated her

The testimonies from the doctors who had met Natuzza Evolo several times over the years are shocking. "I remember it like it was yesterday," said Dr. Umberto Corapi, orthopedic assistant at Lamezia hospital. "I visited Natuzza a few days before Easter, many years ago, and I saw a crown of thorns, I mean a blood crown on her scalp. I was shocked. One of those drops of blood was flowing from one of Natuzza's temples and ended up on the pillow. It was incredible. It was as if an invisible pen were writing the phrase 'Come to me All' in block capitals. I will never forget that episode. Never."

"I have assisted Natuzza Evolo," said Dr. Isa Mantelli, "for two consecutive years, in 1979 and in 1980, always on Good Friday. For three hours, from 12 to 3 in the afternoon, and I remember this woman afflicted by unimaginable pain, who struggled to breathe, as if she were about to suffocate. Eventually, she became cyanotic and she had seizures. Three times. I thought she was going to die, but then she recovered. Slowly."

One day, the doctors focused on a detail that they had not noticed before: "It was on Good Friday, as usual," Dr. Umberto Corapi said, "and we decided to examine her shoulders and we realized that an excoriated hematoma was forming on her right shoulder. From a medical point of view, it was impressive. I remember the color of her shoulder turning into purple until the hematoma was formed. We saw the evolution of that hematoma with our eyes, and it was like a burden on Natuzza's shoulder."

"When she regained consciousness, we asked her many questions, and she replied that she was experiencing the crucifixion of Jesus…" But there is a very important detail that only very few know, something that Natuzza did not like to talk about.

"I went back to Natuzza," said Dr. Mario Cortese, "a few days after the Holy week, and I asked her 'How is the cross carried by Jesus? Does it look like one of the crosses we have in our churches?" Natuzza replied: "Absolutely not, it was completely different. It was like a trunk, like a yoke, and when we got up there, we found the other part already stuck in the ground."

There are countless testimonies like these. Professor Valerio Marinelli, nuclear physicist and Professor Emeritus at the University of Calabria, has catalogued, analyzed, collected, and commented on them in a dozen essays, all on the "Case of Natuzza Evolo", the last of which was recently published and addresses the "bilocation" phenomenon, Natuzza's alleged ability to "travel the world" while remaining in her home in Paravati.

Father Agostino Gemelli condemns Natuzza to isolation

The Archive of *Cattolica University* in Milan has kept confidential correspondence on the case of Natuzza Evolo since 1940.

One of the most mysterious pages in the history of Natuzza Evolo, is the investigation conducted by the official Church of the time in the early months of 1940, after a long series of inexplicable events experienced by Natuzza when she was just a girl and was already working as a servant.

The main concern of the Church at that time was the confidence shown by Natuzza when sharing her conversations with the Virgin Mary with her hosts, and that she seemed to know a lot about the afterlife and the world of the dead, which Natuzza claimed she could get in touch with. The most impressive thing was the detailed descriptions she could give to the relatives of the dead with whom she spoke. She could tell what they were wearing in the coffin after their death. On one occasion, Natuzza was able to tell what color the skirt of a woman who had died twenty years earlier was and even describe its pattern. On another occasion, she described the color and cut of the suit worn by a local notable when he was buried.

In Paravati, the small town where Natuzza was born and lived her entire life, people still remember that number of faithful rushing in her home to ask about their loved ones, to find out if "they were okay", to ask her if "there was something they could do for them". Natuzza had a clear answer for each of them. She never had doubts; she never hesitated when telling the stories of the dead she claimed she could see and talk to. So, you could not help trusting her and her words. She often entered a trance state as well, and, of course, all these strange events were considered suspicious by the official Church.

So, as Natuzza was becoming more and more popular, the Bishop of the Diocese of Mileto, Monsignor Paolo Albera, decided to write a letter directly to Father Agostino Gemelli, to ask him for advice on what to do and to get the final opinion of the Church on the case of Natuzza Evolo. It was February

18, 1940, and Father Agostino Gemelli, founder and rector of *Cattolica University* in Milan, was already considered by the international academic world as one of the most authoritative scientists of the time in Italy: no one could unravel the mystery of that woman who had "blood sweats" better than him.

The following is the full text of the letter that Monsignor Paolo Albera sent to Father Agostino Gemelli in Milan:

"Most Reverend, please forgive me if I am taking the liberty of sending you a dossier on the case of Evolo Fortunata and the strange events that are happening in one of my dioceses; I would like to have your opinion, so that I can soothe the souls of my people."

Monsignor Paolo Albera also attached a detailed report to his letter on what was happening in the house where Natuzza lived, written by a local priest, Don Francesco Pititto, together with an accurate medical report: "The medical report and the testimonies can describe the case better than I could do," concluded Monsignor Paolo Albera. "Thank you for your kind attention. Yours sincerely."

This was the first of many letters that the Rector of *Cattolica University* in Milan and the Bishop of Mileto wrote to each other. On the one hand, there were the diagnoses delivered and the information collected in Calabria, which confirmed the authenticity of Natuzza's events and episodes; while, on the other, the proverbial skepticism of the academic world and scientific research.

Father Agostino Gemelli's reply to Monsignor Paolo Albera was immediate. It is dated February 22, 1940: "Most Reverend – the letter sent by Father Gemelli to the Bishop of Mileto begins with these words – I have received the dossier on the case of Fortunata Evolo. I will analyze it in a few days, and I will provide an accurate opinion. Please, keep me in your prayers and accept my respects."

Meanwhile, Easter arrived, and during Holy Week, Natuzza experienced the same extraordinary and inexplicable events that had made her so popular all over the world: first, the stigmata appeared, then the blood sweats, and the blood flowing from her forehead imprinting images of various kinds on the handkerchiefs used to cleanse her wounds, including letters in Hebrew and drawings of chalices and crosses. At that moment, people started to talk and spread rumors. The young woman who had blood sweats and wounds in her hands and feet became the main subject of every conversation in the town and the surrounding areas.

It was pretty clear that the Bishop did not know how to manage the situation, and did not even know what to say to the many who turned to him to ask how to "read" or interpret the mystery of Paravati. So, he decided to write another letter addressed exclusively to Father Agostino Gemelli, but this time he made a mistake, as instead of writing Fortunata Evolo, Monsignor Albera called Natuzza "Fortunata Evoli" three times.

It was July 8, 1940. This is the full text of the letter sent by the Bishop to the Rector of *Cattolica*: "Most Reverend, I am writing once again with reference to the case of 'Evoli Fortunata', that I kindly asked you to analyze and on which you expressed your authoritative opinion with a note dated February 27. I did what you recommended to do, but since I was not able to stop the rumors, I will report the events so that you can give your valuable opinion. Since June 29, after receiving your comments, Evoli has been experiencing bleeding, cross-shaped skin rashes located on her shoulder and on her chest, left side.

Such bleeding rushes are always preceded and followed by severe chest pain extended to her left shoulder. She is exhausted. The doctor who examined her said that Ms. Evoli is perfectly healthy in every single part of her body, and he cannot explain this phenomenon. I can send her blood-soaked diapers if you ask me to. I am kindly asking for Your authoritative opinion, for which I thank You in advance. Yours sincerely, Paolo Albera, Bishop of Mileto."

Father Gemelli wasted no time, and replied to Monsignor Paolo Albera on July 13, as soon as he received the letter from Calabria. "Most Reverend, analyzing the blood will not give us the answers we are looking for. The only thing to do is to send the woman to a qualified healthcare facility, where she could be properly examined and monitored by specially trained personnel. I am telling you this because I suspect she could suffer from hysteria; this is the first thing to be excluded before determining the nature of the phenomena reported by Your Excellency. We must be careful, and above all do not give too much importance to such phenomena, as usually these patients tend to recover when the events they report are diminished. I would to take this opportunity to send Your Excellency my best regards."

Twenty days later, on August 1, 1940, Monsignor Paolo Albera was ready to write another letter to Father Agostino Gemelli. But, this time, to make sure he wasn't misunderstood, he typed it on the official headed paper of the Bishopric of Mileto. Referring to Father Gemelli's letter dated July 13, Monsignor Paolo Albera repeated the same mistake when he called his "patient" Fortunata Evoli. Actually, the surname was properly spelled on the original text of the letter, but then, perhaps while re-reading the text, Monsignor Albera used his pen to correct it. Unlike the previous letters, which were quite understandable, this time the letter addressed to the Rector of *Cattolica* was quite confused. The description made by Monsignor Paolo Albera of the problem and secondary issues was, in fact, not clear enough. Let's read the document together, starting with the introduction: "In your much appreciated letter dated July 13 – with regard to the case of Evoli Fortunata – you suggested that she could be suffering from hysteria, and that the best thing to do was to send her to a special nursing home where the staff is qualified."

So far so good. Monsignor Paolo Albera confirmed that he attached importance to the diagnosis of hysteria suggested by Father Agostino Gemelli, but this time the Bishop of Mileto introduces a new element, which he had never actually mentioned to the Rector of *Cattolica University*, that is, the risk that Natuzza could become, in the popular imagination, a "Saint". "Now, although, the doctors who visited her are convinced that it is hysteria, and she has lost her reputation, to which her family had contributed…"

What had actually happened in the weeks prior to this letter? Well, Natuzza had announced to her employers – in the house where she had been hired as a servant – that "she would soon pass onto the next life" and she had also specified the date of her death. This piece of information was disseminated, reached the nearby towns and communities, and crossed the regional borders, which was impressive, given the times and that turning local news into matters of national significance was quite difficult. And the fact that Natuzza had predicted the day of her death had already made her almost a "Saint".

In his letter to Father Gemelli, Monsignor Paolo Albera says it clearly: thank God Natuzza is not dead, as this greatly reduces her reputation as a "Saint". "She has lost her reputation, which her family had contributed, since she did pass, as she announced, on July 26, at 2 p.m."

But Monsignor Paolo Albera was still convinced that the problem had not been solved, and in his letter to Father Gemelli he insisted on pointing out the "phenomena of sweats, and not just that", but also the "images created by the blood sweats".

They all seemed to agree, however, on the decision to send Natuzza "to a nursing home, as Your Excellency has kindly suggested, although some doctors say it is not worth it, as these phenomena can all be explained by hysteria, and it would be enough to treat her in a proper facility."

But where to send her? Where to lock her up? And, above all, who to contact? These are questions that Monsignor Paolo Albera had asked himself several times, and it was quite understandable, as the situation was getting out of hand. Monsignor Paolo Albera, in fact, did not have difficulty recognizing that it would not be easy to remove Natuzza from the house where she was living and working, and wrote something to Father Gemelli that perhaps the rector of *Cattolica University* did not expect from such an illuminated and stern bishop: "To give your Excellency an idea of what is going on here, I will tell you what happened. Last July, everybody was talking about this young woman, alluding to the fact that she could be a Saint, and many women from the neighboring towns – and not just those – came to Mileto to ask for her blessing and to resort to her healing powers."

In the previous months, in fact, people had been gathering for days in front of the house where Natuzza lived and worked. People came to Paravati from the most distant towns in the region looking for Natuzza, sometimes just to see her, to deliver a message, but mostly to ask for a grace. Monsignor Paolo Albera explained the whole situation to the Rector of *Cattolica University*, this time also raising some concerns: "... Public Security had to intervene and call for backup to restore public order, together with the Capitano dei Regi Carabinieri, and a commissioner of Public Safety. Today, the area surrounding the house looks like a desert, as she did not die as she had predicted, so she has lost her credibility with these good people. Please, tell me the name of the health facility you want to send her to. And please, send me once again your valuable advice and forgive me for bothering You with my questions. I am sure our Dear Lord will reward your efforts. I will pray and ask God to bless you for your much appreciated work. Yours sincerely, Paolo Albera."

He did not have to wait long for Father Gemelli's response. On August 9, 1940, with the registration number 6395 clearly visible at the top of his letter, the Rector of *Cattolica University* wrote to the Bishop of Mileto recognizing that "Things such as those Your Excellency reported to me always cause pain to a Bishop. This has already happened in many other unfortunate cases similar to this one."

This time, Father Gemelli went straight to the point when he suggested a final solution to the Evolo case: "In principle the solution is always the same: isolation, so that people can finally forget what happened."

So, Natuzza had to be isolated from the rest of the world. Father Gemelli had no doubts about it; he is, in fact, more than certain that there is no other solution to tarnish the "myth" of this young woman from Calabria. But Father Gemelli went far beyond the pure concept of "isolation" and advised the Bishop of Mileto to "forbid the priests and members of the *Azione Cattolica* to take an interest her, or they would pay the consequences." Something that sounded like the "Holy Inquisition", but reading between the lines, we can see how those letters written by Father Gemelli to Monsignor Paolo Albera were full of "anger" and "intolerance" towards the reported events. Father Gemelli also advised the Bishop of Mileto to immediately remove Natuzza from the house where she lived: "Possibly remove her from her comfort zone and send her somewhere else, where she cannot exercise her powers."

And to avoid any misunderstandings, the Rector of *Cattolica University* was even harsher: "It's pointless sending Ms. Evoli to a health facility, as the doctors have already confirmed that she suffers from hysteria". It was pretty clear that Father Gemelli did not want to hear more about the case of Natuzza Evolo – or Evoli, as he insisted on calling her. On other occasions, and in cases similar to this one, Father Gemelli would leave Milan to see the person involved, but this time he thought it was pointless and perhaps even unnecessary, and he felt the need to justify his choice, although he did not sound very credible: "I am not saying I do not want to do it; indeed, I would be more than happy to come, if necessary, if Your Excellency asks me to; but maybe we could save money this time, which is not a secondary aspect to consider." Then, he added: "I would ask You to send the woman here, in Milan, so that she could live in a religious house for an affordable rate, but less money does not mean no money at all."

The bottom line was Natuzza had to stay in Calabria, case closed. "Since I don't know the local situation," Father Gemelli insisted, "I am not sure Your Excellency can send Ms. Evoli to isolation; people who are close to her could accuse You of 'kidnapping' her, rights violations, and things like this. Something that has already happened in some cases. Anyway, this is my opinion and I hope Your Excellency will appreciate it. Please, send me a letter if you have any questions, and I will answer them. Bending down to kiss Your Sacred Ring, I send your Excellency my best regards."

So, according to the eminent founder of *Cattolica University*, the case of "Fortunata Evoli" should be immediately closed!

"No mystery, then". "No transcendence". "We are dealing with an ordinary case of hysteria. That's it."

Father Agostino Gemelli clearly blamed the incompetence of the doctors who had examined Natuzza in Calabria and used his charisma as a scientist to convince Monsignor Paolo Albera to bury the whole story. "Enough with the interrogations", "Enough with the exorcisms to redeem that young woman". All this would only worsen her "condition". And from that moment, the Bishop of Mileto did everything he could to follow the instructions received from Milan.

The witnessed miracles performed by Natuzza in the mental institution

Today, Father Gemelli's report would be considered not just baseless, superficial, and almost irrational, but also – from a scientific point of view – quite in contrast with scientific knowledge.

Valerio Marinelli – a university professor and a nuclear engineer much appreciated in the academic world – says it without ambiguity in his first book on Natuzza.

With regard to the analysis conducted by Father Gemelli, Valerio Marinelli is very explicit, and as a scientist he points out: "I have never heard of people suffering from hysteria – be they illiterate or educated – who have experienced the phenomenon of spontaneous blood writings. Affirming that hemography is caused by hysteria makes no sense and has no scientific basis."

Valerio Marinelli goes even further, when he adds: "You don't have to be that smart to reject the opinion given by the Founder of *Cattolica*, I mean, the idea that the visions experienced by the mystic from Paravati were due to hysteria. Because, if in principle visions can be associated with hallucinations, Natuzza proved the consistency of her apparitions, providing details of the entities she could see that were so accurate that even the most skeptical should be convinced."

In a nutshell, Father Gemelli was completely wrong.

Of course, after receiving clear instructions from the Rector of *Cattolica University*, Monsignor Paolo Albera, bishop of Mileto, didn't have much choice: he had to listen to that eminent scientist. And so, immediately after the summer of 1940, on the morning of September 2, a new life began for Natuzza Evolo.

Natuzza marries Pasquale Nicolace and gives birth to five children

After a complex and even "quite tormented" consultation, the bishop of Mileto decided to have Natuzza locked up in a mental institution in Reggio Calabria. This was eventually the best solution that the bishop of Mileto could find to follow the instructions received from Father Agostino Gemelli.

As the scholars remind us, the exact same thing had happened to Padre Pio twenty years earlier.

In fact, when he was asked to give his opinion on the case of the friar from Pietrelcina, Father Gemelli had warned the doctors who had examined him in San Giovanni Rotondo: "Be careful, he is a self-mutilating psychopath". And then again: "Monitor him, and if you can, isolate him".

History repeats itself.

But this story is full of twists and turns. Once she was locked up in a mental institution in Reggio Calabria, a new life began for Natuzza, quite difficult at first, and in some ways also "violent", as putting a young woman like her into a mental institution was, indeed, something of "unprecedented violence", and a choice that made no sense from any point of view.

She mentioned that experience several times – when she was still alive – and those very few times that she had agreed to talk about it, she had also found the strength to smile.

In the mental institution, however, those extraordinary phenomena that characterized her entire life until the day of her death, including blood sweats, did not stop.

When she was locked up, in fact, Natuzza repeatedly experienced the mystery of blood flowing from her forehead, chest, shoulder, and knees, and she also continued to have her extraordinary visions, talk to the Virgin Mary, and "meet" the dead. She provided very accurate descriptions of the souls in purgatory, or the angels of heaven, and she "traveled" the world without ever leaving her homeland. The latter is what anthropologists call the "bilocation" phenomenon, also investigated by physicist Valerio Marinelli in one of his most valuable essays.

All this clearly had an impact on the relationships that Natuzza had with the nuns who took care of her, although she was in a mental institution, and also with the doctors and nurses working there, who no longer saw her a "a psychiatric patient" or as a person under surveillance. They began to show her respect, as they were amazed by all those extraordinary and paranormal phenomena.

Even the nuns turned to her to ask for the "grace of Our Lady", and the employees of the facility frequently visited her to ask if she had "news" from their loved ones who had passed away.

In short, Natuzza became a "legend" even there, in a mental institution, and she revolutionized the lives of all the people in that facility.

The first to realize what was happening was the director of the institution, Prof. Annibale Puca, who finally decided that the best thing to do was to send Natuzza back home as soon as possible.

Surprisingly, when the doctor called her to tell her that "she could finally go home" as there was no longer any reason for her to stay in Reggio Calabria, Natuzza told Professor Puca that she wanted to become a nun,
and remain in that hospital forever with the "sisters who loved her so much."

But the old psychiatrist was not moved. Indeed, he believed that the ideal solution for her was a normal life, and the day her closest relatives arrived in Reggio Calabria to take Natuzza back to Paravati, he advised them to help Natuzza find a man and get married.

"Natuzza must get married", "Find her a husband", "She is a woman, and she needs to become a mother", "With the support of her children, she will be able to recover", as "this is perhaps the only way for her to live a normal life."

So, after spending two months in Reggio, Calabria, Natuzza left the psychiatric hospital and went back to her town, where, a few months later, she married a man with whom she shared the rest of her life: Pasquale Nicolace, a local carpenter.

Arranged marriage was not uncommon in Reggio Calabria in those years; indeed, it was quite normal, like proxy marriage. Later, Natuzza became the mother of five children: Salvatore, Antonio, Anna Maria, Angela and Francesco Nicolace.

However, contrary to what the psychiatrist had imagined and predicted, Natuzza Evolo continued to experience those extraordinary and inexplicable phenomena that had brought her to the mental institution, until she died.

Natuzza Evolo

Extraordinary and scientifically unexplained healings; diagnoses delivered in great detail; handkerchiefs used to wipe her body imprinted with her blood; stigmata on her hands and feet; thorn wounds on her forehead; conversations with the dead; simultaneous appearances in different parts of the world; a wonderful scent of flowers announcing her presence while she continued to live and stay in her home in Calabria; followers and faithful everywhere; and visions of and conversations with the Virgin Mary. Natuzza Evolo was all of this.

"...I am only an earthworm ..."

"Our Lady appeared to me for the first time fifty-five years ago to tell me that soon I would have a bigger house where I could receive Her... I remember that day as if it was yesterday. And I remember Her radiant face, how calm she was when she looked at me and talked to me ... I felt like I had already met her a thousand times before that day; she was glowing, she was stretching her hands out to me and gazing at a nearby clearing. Sometime later I saw her again ... she told me that she wanted a large church to rise here, and that it should be called the 'Immaculate Heart of Mary Refuge of souls' ..."

In one of the last interviews that Natuzza Evolo gave to RAI, the mystic from Paravati talked about the day when Our Lady appeared to her for the first time and asked her to do her best to build a large church in front of her old country house. She was incredibly calm, and she described what happened in great detail. Today - almost 60 years from that day, and after her death - Paravati has its own Basilica that will soon be consecrated and will become a place of worship and a major pilgrimage site, as Natuzza had always dreamed of.

Those who were in Paravati a little less than a year ago, on the Day of the Dead, have surely understood how much this poor Calabrian peasant has left to others, with her example and earthly presence. Twenty thousand faithful from all over the world came to celebrate her, and, above all to pray at her tomb on the anniversary of her death. The sons of hope, people who have had a strong relationship with Paravati and with Natuzza's house, and who will never forget her.

Anyone who wants to listen to Natuzza's words can find her on the internet. Thousands of people search for her name on Youtube every day to see her again and talk to her, maybe ask her something, and there are many videos taken from her television interviews.

Natuzza Evolo's life is like a fairytale.

Don Michele Cordiano, one of the priests who was closest to her in her last years, uses these words to describe her, and does so with tears in his eyes, because Natuzza was more than a mother to him:

"Natuzza was born on August 23, 1924, in Paravati, a hamlet of Mileto, a town with three thousand inhabitants in the province of Vibo Valentia, Calabria. She never met her father, Fortunato, as – a few months before her birth – he left for Argentina and never came back. Her mother, Maria Angela Valente, did with what she had to raise her children and did her best to get them food, but sometimes it was little Natuzza – whose real name was Fortunata – who had to beg the baker for some bread. So, the situation was precarious, and she did not go to school, also because she had to look after her brothers".

But when did Natuzza begin to experience the first extraordinary phenomena?

Michele Cordiano is unstoppable: "Natuzza was only eight years old when San Francesco di Paola, the great Calabrian saint, the patron saint of seafarers, appeared to her for the first time. Since this was absolutely normal to her, Natuzza reported this episode to her family, and her confidence started to raise concerns in the small community. That was just the beginning. When Natuzza received her First Communion, she realized that she had blood in her mouth, and she swallowed it. Then, terrified at the thought of "eating Jesus" and of committing sin, she told everyone, but the parish priest reassured her.

"These were the first signs of something extraordinary, and such events became more frequent a few years later when, towards the end of 1938, Natuzza was hired as a servant for the family of a lawyer in Mileto whose name was Silvio Colloca. At that time, Natuzza was an obedient, shy, and smart girl who could complete housework very quickly; that's why she was much appreciated by Mr. Colloca".

Is it true that this is where she experienced the second extraordinary event in her life?

"One afternoon, when Mrs. Alba Colloca was offering a cup of coffee to her guests, Natuzza spontaneously asked her why she hadn't offered coffee to the priest too. 'Sorry, but what priest?', the lady asked. 'The one who is sitting with the other two gentlemen,' she replied. The lady returned to the living room, reported the episode and one of the two guests said that her brother, who had died years earlier, was a priest. They called Natuzza and she described him in great detail. No doubt it was him.

Another day, they heard her whisper, "Be careful with those glasses, or Mrs. Colloca will scold me!" The lady asked her who she was talking to, and she replied that she was talking to some angels who had come to visit her. At the age of fifteen, she returned to the house of the Colloca family after receiving Confirmation, and she realized that her shirt was wet. So, she took it off and she found a large cross of blood on the inside of her shirt.

Don Michele smiles. "Do you really think that the Colloca house has become the house of the spirits over time?" And yet, the family where Natuzza was serving started to raise concerns.

"One evening, during dinner, Mr. and Mrs. Colloca were talking quietly and discussing what to do with that girl who was so good but also so strange. They concluded that she had to get back to her home in Paravati. But, when Mrs. Colloca entered Natuzza's room to talk to her, she found her in tears. Natuzza was sobbing and crying, and she told her, "A lady came to visit me, it was your mother, and she told me that you want to kick me out of this house!"

Mrs. Colloca reassured her, although she had already decided what to do. But the next day, Natuzza asked her: "Why does your mother have a hoarse voice?"

Mrs. Colloca almost fainted, as her mother had throat cancer and had died a few years earlier, so she really had a hoarse voice (*abracatizza,* in dialect*).* And when she showed her a photo of her mother, Natuzza had no doubts: "Yes, this is the woman who came to visit me last night."

Stigmata and blood sweat, the ordeal of Natuzza Evolo

According to Francesco Mesiano, one of the first scholars to approach the story of Natuzza Evolo, she was very young when she experienced visions and other mystic phenomena for the first time. She was a woman who could see the dead and talk to them, who could enter a trance state, who had blood sweats – which were more evident during the Lent – and who also experienced the great mystery of the stigmata. The blood that flowed from her wounds, in contact with bandages or handkerchiefs, produced the hemographic phenomenon: blood writings and strange signs that were hard to interpret, texts of prayers in different languages, images of chalices, hosts, the Virgin Mary, hearts, crowns of thorns… it was a real mystery. A mystery that, after her death, has not been revealed, and is preserved in the Vatican coffers, where today the case of Natuzza Evolo is being analyzed and studied in detail. In 1941, Natuzza left the Colloca family and moved into her maternal grandmother's house.

Her plan was to become a nun, but soon she realized that she was too poor, and that those strange phenomena she was experiencing would disturb the peace of any convent. So, she decided to get married. On January 14, 1944, Natuzza married Pasquale Nicolace, a carpenter from Paravati, and a new life began for her. The young couple moved to a very poor little house in the old town, which, over the years, has become the true and only silent witness of her visions, conversations, confessions, meetings, and deliveries of messages from the afterlife. Five children were born, Salvatore, Antonio, Anna Maria, Angela, and Francesco, who are now all happily married. Eleven grandchildren and three great-grandchildren still pray at her grave.

On the day of her funeral, thousands of people from all over the world came to Paravati, people who had met the woman afflicted by the stigmata, people who believed they had been summoned by her, on what was probably the happiest day of her life.

A long line formed in front of her coffin including many women, priests, young people, girls holding the hands of older women, their mothers, aunts, grandmothers, sisters. Different generations from five different continents flooding in a clearing that was once just a clay quarry, and that was about to house one of the largest basilicas in Europe.

But no one was crying on that day. Natuzza's funeral was like a feast, a common prayer, a hymn to life. Sixty years later, her prayer groups met again in the same place where the Virgin Mary appeared to Natuzza to ask her to build her church there.

Natuzza used to receive her guests in a small room, and she always wore black. When someone entered the room, she soon asked the reason for that visit ... and all guests immediately connected with her.

Many came just to see her, to exchange a few words with her, many did not even know what to ask her. They talked to her about their children, husbands, parents, work ... and she listened to everyone without saying a word. Then she would deliver her prayer message.

Many came out of that room with tears in their eyes; others seemed to be glowing or swore they would be back as soon as possible. A mystery that not even the scholars and scientists who came to Paravati from all over the world managed to explain.

Pino Nano meets Natuzza Evolo for the first (but not the last) time

"I see your guardian angel." These were the first words pronounced by Natuzza the first time I met her for an interview.

Natuzza, if you were asked to describe yourself, what would you answer?
"I would tell the truth, and I would say that I am just a poor woman. Just an earthworm ..."

But they say you have the power to perform miracles ...
"They say many things about me, but the fact that I can perform miracles is the most inaccurate thing that can be said, or supposed ... I have never performed a single miracle in my entire life."

Yet, there are thousands of people who came here from all over the world and who would swear they received a miracle from you ...
"The truth is that I have never performed miracles. I have only prayed for the personal tragedies of thousands of people. People who came to me from all over the world. Sometimes, truly desperate people. What I can do is pray, pray to the Lord to have mercy on them, help them deal with her tragedies and suffering. I pray because God wants me to pray for others. That's what I am here for."

There are many people who came to you for the first time and to whom you delivered an accurate diagnosis without even knowing them: how is it possible?
"It wasn't me. It was the guardian angel – we all have a guardian angel behind us – who suggested the things to say to the people who come to visit me."

Natuzza, sometimes you deliver diagnoses using the same scientific terms used by the most famous doctors in the world: don't you think this is something absolutely extraordinary?
"But it is not me who makes extraordinary things happen. I just repeat what my angel suggests me to say, and sometimes I repeat things I cannot even understand."

But why do you say that it is your guardian angel who suggests you the things to say?
"Because this is exactly what happens. Behind each of us there is a guardian angel who lives with us, who follows us, and who knows everything about us. When a person comes to me and his or her guardian angel suggests things to report to that person, I just repeat those things."

But is it true that once a priest in plain clothes came to you and you recognized him immediately?
"I remember that day pretty well: as soon as I saw this gentleman enter my house, I went to him and kissed his hand. I remember that he was amazed, he asked me if I had been informed of the fact that he was a priest. I told him that I saw his guardian angel on his left. That was how I recognized him, as all other people have their guardian angel on their right. At first he was stunned, then told me that he was not wearing clerical clothing because he wanted to talk more freely about some stuff."

Natuzza, do you remember the day when Our Lady appeared to you for the first time?
"How can I forget it? I remember that I was still a child, and Our Lady came to see me several times after that day; every time she said something to me, things that came true."

What do you talk about when She appears to you?
"Well, we talk about the things that happened to me during the day. I tell her about the people who come to visit me, I thank her for the strength that the Lord gives me every day. Every day I meet at least three hundred people in this house, only the Lord can give me the support I need to do it. And then I share the terrible stories of those people with Our Lady. Thousands of families suffering because of some problems they are dealing with."

How does Our Lady appear to you?
"She looks like a young woman; she could be sixteen, seventeen at the most, and she is beautiful, regal, and extraordinarily proud. She has beautiful eyes and long, loose hair."

Have you ever asked her for a grace?
"Whenever she appears to me, I always ask her something. And she does answer to me. I realize it later, when a lot of people come back to me and tell me that their problems have been finally solved. This is how I know that Our Lady and the Lord listen to my prayers."

Natuzza, some people claim to have seen you sweat blood several times ...
"Not just some. Thousands of people in these years have seen me sweat blood. It is one of those mysteries that I have been experiencing for years, but no one has been able to explain it."

Is it true that the blood on your forehead is often formed into writings and images upon handkerchiefs or bandages?
"Yes, it is, and this is also something that cannot be explained. A lot of people, after wiping away my sweat, found strange images and drawings, including crosses, on their handkerchiefs... I don't know why."

There are also those who would swear they had received a visit from you at their homes, even in Argentina, on the other side of the world, yet you have never left this town...
"It is neither a feeling nor an illusion. It is just the truth. I often leave my house spiritually to meet people, bring a message, report things ... It is true, I can do it. Without leaving my house ... "

Is it true that this phenomenon – bilocation, as experts call it – is anticipated by an intense scent of flowers?
"That's what people say ..."

Natuzza, you never went to school, but there are people who swear they heard you speak foreign languages, such as German, Spanish, Greek, Hebrew ...

"Yes, but I'm not really speaking other languages when this happens. I am just repeating what the guardian angel tells me and asks me to repeat. German people came to me, and we were able to understand each other perfectly. Again, I cannot speak foreign languages, it's my guardian angel who suggests what to say to those people..."

Do you have an idea of the number of people who have been to your house?
"Thousands of people, hundreds of thousands, almost three hundred people a day, sometimes even more, especially when I was younger".

What do you say to those people?
"I pray. If someone asks me something, and his or her guardian angel helps me better understand the problem reported to me, then I say something."

How did you manage to see so many people?
"I've been receiving so many people for more than fifty years now, yet I've always been there for my family. I used to get up early in the morning, around 4:00, and take care of the house until 7:00. Then, I started to receive the people who came here, and I never went to bed before midnight. I have burned our food a couple of times, but I have always been there for my family."

When you talk to these people, do you ever have the feeling that they do not believe you?
"I didn't ask them to come. Everyone is free to believe and, if they want to, to pray. The best thing for a woman like me is to see a lot of people come back to tell me that my prayer has comforted them."

Have you ever predicted someone's future?
"No, never. It's something I've never done, and I'll never do."

Have you ever seen heaven?
"I met some souls who are in heaven, and they were happy, free, radiant, surrounded by a beautiful wheat field ..."

But you know life after death. There are those who say that you can talk to the dead ...

"Sometimes I meet souls who beg me to bring messages to their families. And I meet happy souls, those who have the privilege of living in heaven, and unhappy souls, those who live in purgatory."

How can you talk to the dead?
"Many people come to me and show me the photographs of their loved ones who passed: sometimes I have the pleasure to meet those souls, who ask me to bring messages to their relatives. I do not see all of them, of course. But when I do, I tell their relatives."

Natuzza, is it true that you always tell the people who come to visit you that you are a happy woman?
"True, I am happy, as our Lord gave me more than I have ever expected or dreamed of. Many people come to me and confess to me that they are hopeless because their sons suffer from a very serious condition: my children are healthy, and I'm a lucky woman. I know that Our Lord is the reason why I'm so lucky, and I am deeply grateful to him for this. How could I not be a happy woman? Or do you really believe, as many do, that material goods raise happiness?

So, everything is going incredibly well, isn't it?
"Life is much more than material values. Everything dies, and what remains is what we have been able to build inside us. Only prayer can help us overcome the idea that money and wealth can bring joy ... Thousands of sad people have come to this house, and I learned from them that money or wealth cannot soothe a sad soul ... Every time I pray I think about other people, and I pray to the Lord to give men the peace they need to go on with their lives."

Have you ever tried to make an analysis of your life?
"Who hasn't? Each of us, at some point, makes an analysis, and if you do not have something to offer yourself, in your heart, or if you have not been able to build anything in your life, whether it is for yourself and for the others, then you'll find out that you are a failure ... money is just an illusion, just like wealth. Faith in God and our ability to love other people are the only things that matter."

Before I leave, can I ask you what life has taught you so far?

"Something beautiful. The certainty that God really exists, and that nothing is more powerful than his love. God exists. This is wonderful and extraordinary. This is all I know. And it's something I cannot explain. I cannot read the numbers or the letters of the alphabet, but I can say to those people who keep coming to see me that praying is worth it, because it is the only way to understand the true meaning of life. And if we don't understand it, life after death will be even sadder than this one."

I suppose, then, that death is the only thing that doesn't scare you ...
"Why should it scare me? Death is the natural solution to our existence. With no death there would be no us, and there would be no life. If there is life, there can be death. Those who believe that death is the end if everything are wrong; it is only the beginning of a new journey. I realized it when I was still a child: one day a beggar come to my house, a house where there was only some bread; I opened the bench where we usually kept the bread, and I gave that one piece of bread that was left to that poor man...

Before he left, he asked me if I had a wish to fulfill, I told him that I wanted to meet San Francesco di Paola. He smiled at me and said, "Today your wish has come true." I have never seen that man again, but in my dreams, I've asked him for things that came true ... that day I realized that San Francesco di Paola had come to see me, and that death is just the triumph of earthly life ... after death there is another life in which we will finally see the ones we loved and that we have lost again."

-As soon as Natuzza Evolo died, people cried out for her sainthood, and after ten years, the Roman Catholic Church initiated the process of her beatification, after the necessary preliminary investigations. Natuzza died at the age of 85 in her home in Paravati on November 1, 2009, and on April 6, 2019, the bishop of the diocese of Mileto-Nicotera-Tropea, Monsignor Luigi Renzo, officially announced that her beatification process had been initiated. A young intellectual from the Cosenza church, Don Enzo Gabrieli, was appointed postulator and the news of her imminent beatification spread around the globe.

The real miracles performed by Natuzza are those revealed by the people she met

I remember the day I met Natuzza for the first time like it was yesterday...

It was early in the afternoon. A young lady came to visit her, she was from Taranto, and I remember the moment these two women met perfectly well. It was a very moving moment, almost hard to describe and to imagine. It was like they had known each other for long time; the silence was broken by the tears of that young woman who looked desperate. It was like she had been waiting for that moment to finally cry in Natuzza's arms. I have never known if she was crying because of the burden of a terrible tragedy, or if she had finally managed to overcome a difficult situation.

So, I waited for her to calm down, then I approached that young lady and asked her why she was so moved.

This was the answer she gave me: "A few years ago I was in Paris. I ended up at the *Hôpital Pitié Salpêtrièren*, one of the largest hospitals in Paris, as my father had cancer, and the situation was pretty bad. I had come to Paris just to see if there was something that could be done to add just a few days to his life, which was about to come to an end. At least, this was what the Italian doctors had told us. And one day, in the afternoon, at the entrance to the ward where my father was hospitalized, I met Natuzza. She told me that she came from far away, from a region similar to mine – I came from Puglia, she was from Calabria – so, I told her that I was there because of my father, while she said she was there to offer her support to "a person she cared a lot about."

"After speaking about everything and anything, Natuzza caressed me, just under my neck. I could feel her love in that gesture, and I remember that I let this woman touch me where I had been feeling something for a while; a lump, maybe, but I hadn't given that much importance. After she caressed me – I remember – Natuzza looked into my eyes and begged me to seek medical attention. She immediately told me that she had felt something under my neck, where she had caressed me, maybe just a cyst, but she could not tell.

"The first thing I thought was that, with her gesture and her words, this poor woman wanted to show that she cared about me, or maybe it was just her way to suggest to take care of me, as I was so young. Who knew?

"At first I let it go, I tried to forget her and her advice, but it was not easy. Every time I met her again, Natuzza did nothing but repeat what she had already told me, 'see a doctor!', 'don't waste your time', she insisted.

"So, one morning, at her insistence, I decided to ask the doctors at the hospital."

The diagnosis was shocking. The doctors in Paris had discovered that this young woman had a swollen gland at the height of her thyroid, and after examining her and analyzing the fluid they had extracted they had found out that she had an invasive tumor. "Cancer!"

The woman was rushed into the OR, while her father, compared to her, seemed to have completely recovered.

Two months later, the doctors in Paris had reassured her. They explained that she had arrived just in time for surgery. Two more weeks, they said, and it would be too late for her. But, when they had asked her how she had found out that she was seriously ill, this woman had not been able to give them any plausible answer.

She pretended not to understand their question; she smiled, then she ran to the travel agency and booked a flight to Lamezia Terme. Before arriving in Puglia, at her home, she wanted to visit Paravati, because she had met Natuzza in her dreams, and Natuzza had asked her to come to see her in Paravati.

I have had the pleasure to hear thousands of incredible stories like this one during the years I spent investigating the case of Natuzza Evolo on behalf of RAI. Incredible, mysterious, comparable, recurring, cyclical stories, each more beautiful, more moving, more engaging, but also more tragic than the other.

Monsignor Domenico Tarcisio Cortese, the priest who changed Natuzza's life

There is a priest – or rather a bishop – who has played a key role in Natuzza's life. It is Monsignor Domenico Tarcisio Cortese, bishop of the Diocese of Mileto-Nicotera-Tropea. In fact, he had to deal with Natuzza for thirty years, burdening himself with what was a big and unsolvable issue for the Church of the time, and he accompanied her throughout her amazing journey until the day of her death.

"I was bishop of the diocese of Mileto-Nicotera-Tropea for twenty-eight years, and I can say I'm the chief witness of the events that have marked my long episcopate, having known Natuzza for years. With this contribution," as Monsignor Cortese writes in his afterword to the essay written by Luciano Regolo, Deputy Editorial Director of *Famiglia Cristiana*, and dedicated to her, "I do not intend to judge the extraordinary phenomena attributed to the mystic from Paravati. Only the Church can decide on this delicate matter, when and how it deems appropriate. What I can say for sure is that Natuzza, a woman of faith, did obey the Church, even in the most delicate and difficult moments of her life.

I can confirm it. Some members of the clergy had doubts about Natuzza, because of her visions and her messages, which were sometimes veiled accusations against the clergy. This has caused misunderstandings. When I joined the diocese, in 1979, Natuzza came to me and said: "Your Excellency, if you want me not to receive people and not to talk to them, I will obey you!" I pointed out that I did not have the power, nor did I intend to prevent her from receiving and talking to people, as I believed that her meetings and her words would only do good. She was relieved when she left."

Monsignor Domenico Tarcisio Cortese continued to repeat these words while he was alive: "As a bishop, I have never heard such a loyal declaration of obedience. Natuzza was a woman of faith, and she had much in common with other exceptional witnesses of our time. Padre Pio, for example."

But I prefer to talk about Don Primo Mazzolari. Seen as a frontier priest, too innovative and therefore troublesome, he was rebuked and warned several times by the ecclesiastical authorities, which he never stopped obeying. Today, there is much consensus around the testimony given by this strong and brave man. Before dying, he wrote in his will: "I am sorry if I made my superiors suffer; it was not my intention, but I do not regret having suffered." Pope Paul VI indirectly responded to his statements, almost as if he wanted to ask don Primo forgiveness for what the ecclesiastical authorities had done to him: "Of course, we could not share his ideas. It was hard to keep up with him. He was ahead of his time, he suffered, and we suffered too."

Wherever he went and whenever he was asked about Natuzza or what he thought of her, the old bishop of Mileto always told the same strange story, which gave a clear idea of the great connection they had: "Since she was a girl, Natuzza has always proven her faith, even with extraordinary signs that can be intriguing and disturbing at the same time. Natuzza was a simple and humble woman. There is, in particular, an episode that confirms that Natuzza was a genuine person, but she was also naive. She ordered a statue of the Virgin Mary – with specific features required by her – from Ortisei. Before the statue was blessed so that it could be displayed for veneration by the faithful, I asked to see it. I was just curious. So, one evening, I went to Natuzza's house, and I saw this statue with a young and smiling face and her arms stretched wide in welcome. Then, I said to myself, *this is the first time I see a statue of the Immaculate Conception with its arms stretched out towards other people, and not to Heaven, as if it wants to embrace humanity.*

Natuzza was impatient to hear my views, so she finally asked the question: 'Your Excellency, do you like my statue?" "Yes", I replied, "I definitely like it, but it's not my Virgin Mary." I was joking, but Natuzza did not get it, so she insisted: "How does your Virgin Mary look like?" I should point out that I am a faithful follower of Saint Francis of Assisi, and, according to the Franciscan iconography, the Virgin Mary always holds the Christ Child in her arms. But I didn't waste time reassuring Natuzza. I told her that her Virgin Mary was like Our Lady of Lourdes and of Fatima, who does not hold the Christ Child in her arms, although the 'Blessed Mother' had the Holy Rosary in her hands.

Natuzza, finally reassured, kissed my hand, and said: "Your Excellency, I'm so happy!"

She was an extraordinary woman of faith, that's why she was misunderstood and even scorned by some members of the clergy. And she suffered, but she never stopped obeying the Church, supported by her unshakable faith, and she continued doing what she was doing because she had a mission to accomplish: bringing all the love she could into the world.

Of significance – Bishop Cortese concluded in his interview with the Deputy Editorial Director of *Famiglia Cristiana* – is the confession made by one of Natuzza's children in front of his mother's coffin on the day of her funeral. It was raining buckets and it was also a windy day, and thousands and thousands of faithful were there.

He sounded confident, although he was suffering and he was moved, and he said: "Thank you mom, because, since I was a child, I've always known that I have a family – you, dad, and my four brothers, but I also have many other brothers and sisters, as love can be everywhere in the world. And it was you who taught me this."

Valerio Marinelli, the nuclear engineer who became the official biographer of Natuzza Evolo

Valerio Marinelli has written twelve books on Natuzza Evolo. No one knows the Evolo case better than him, and today he can be considered the only great official biographer of the woman who "could talk to the dead" and had the stigmata.

Valerio Marinelli was born in Rosarno, Calabria, on May 9, 1942, and graduated in Nuclear Engineering at *Politecnico di Torino* in 1967. From 1969 to 1975, he worked as a researcher at the *Centro Studi Nucleari della Casaccia* of CNEN, currently ENEA. He quit his university job on November 1, 2012, but he is still considered as a major academic at the *Campus di Arcavacata*. A man who, with his work and research, has made a great contribution to the University of Calabria. With his impressive curriculum vitae, this man could intimidate anyone (including me), but luckily he knew how to put me at ease: "You can call me Valerio, if you want," he said with a big smile on his face.

Let's start from the beginning, Professor. How did you come up with the idea of dealing with the case of Natuzza Evolo, and when did it happen? When did you meet her for the first time?
At the end of 1975, after working as a researcher for seven years at the *Centro Studi Nucleari della Casaccia* (Rome), I returned to Calabria as I was hired as a professor at the University of Arcavacata. After I arrived at the University of Cosenza, I heard about Natuzza for the first time; it was said that she could "see and talk to Jesus", to the Virgin Mary, and to the dead; that she had experienced the extraordinary phenomena of hemography, bilocation, and stigmata. I had unsolved issues with faith at the time. I grew up in a Catholic family, but during my years as a university student, I had lost my faith and I was not sure if God really existed. However, I was convinced that the case of Natuzza Evolo, if investigated in detail, could prove the existence of God, so I decided to be involved and maybe do something useful for me and for other people.

The first thing I did was reading the book *I fenomeni paranormali di Natuzza Evolo* by Francesco Mesiano and interviewing some witnesses that were still alive. Then, in 1977, I personally went to Natuzza's house, and I suggested she use her gift of bilocation to come and see me at the University of Calabria. The idea was to record a video with some of my colleagues, so that we could study that phenomenon. At the time I was only 35, and I was quite resourceful and confident. Of all the stories I had been told, I was particularly interested in bilocation as, in my opinion, and according to some theologians and scholars, the ability to bilocate is a remarkable proof of the existence of the soul, which is certainly not a physical body. Natuzza told me that bilocation did not depend on her, and that it was God who decided when and where this had to happen. She also explained that God would not allow me to test her.

However, she told me that if I wanted to, I could interview some witnesses of that phenomenon. Later, she confessed that, on that day, her guardian angel predicted to her that I would write some books about her. After meeting Natuzza, I felt even more willing to investigate the case, and, in my free time, I began to travel all over Calabria, as well as outside the region, to interview and ask questions to the people who had dealt with her, and who could confirm her powers.

So, I discovered that Natuzza had advised, comforted, supported, and helped – in many ways – thousands of people and that, apart from her important mystic gifts, she was and continued to be a point of reference and a lifeline for so many people who were suffering and needed help and solidarity. She helped them through grief. She showed them a way to overcome tragedies. I soon found the answers to my questions, and Natuzza gave me the certainty of faith! I thought it was important to leave a trace of her work, through my studies and books.

What do you remember about her? What were your feelings when you had the pleasure to talk to her? How would you describe her?
Those who had the pleasure to meet Natuzza – including me – all had the same feeling: she was a simple, peaceful, and compassionate woman, who was reconciled with God and others.

Twelve books about Natuzza... so many! How to read them? Or rather, how should they be classified?
When, in 1980, I published my first book, *Natuzza di Paravati*, I thought my work on the subject was over, because my research had concluded that those phenomena were real and that Natuzza was telling the truth. But, when I brought her my book, she said: "I apologize for what I am about to tell you, but it's the angel who is suggesting it: this book is not strong enough. But what you wrote is true!"

So, I realized that the spiritual aspects of Natuzza had been not addressed, and I told her that I would work on a second edition of the book. However, she told me not to change my first book, and suggested I write a second book. So, my second book, which took almost five years to complete, focuses more on Natuzza's spirituality, her inner gifts, and her conversion work. I already felt very attached to this woman who had become so important to me, and I continued to note down new events that concerned her. New testimonies were added, and book after book, I created a sort of serialized biography, commenting on the main events of her life almost in real time. Ten volumes in total. The last one contains evidence of what she was able to do even after her death.

Twelve different books, a single structure?
All the volumes have a similar structure: each of them contains a biography, information, testimonies, and documents discussed in chapters often having the same title, in order to make it easier to approach and study the various aspects of Natuzza's personality and charism. For example, all my books contain a chapter on her celestial visions and conversations, a chapter on hemography, the mystical phenomena experienced by her, visions of the dead, etc. They can be considered as a database available to other authors interested in the subject. They also contain all her interviews, including those she had with Pino Nano for RAI.

If you could go back, would you do it again? I mean, ten volumes...
Yes, definitely, even more but I have a job and family, so it's impossible.

How many other times have you seen and talked to Natuzza?
I was lucky enough to see her frequently, especially before she asked those who wished to see her to make an appointment on the phone, when you could go there whenever you wanted and ask all the questions you had.

What was the most impressive thing about her?
She was a very humble person, she has never abused her power, she chose her words with care, and she was sweet, which helped her hide her great personality; I could immediately tell that she did everything she could for other people.

Have you ever questioned the "phenomena" she claimed she was experiencing?
Since I met her, never. A few times her answers left me puzzled, but then, when I asked the question a second time as I needed more clarifications, her answers were always comprehensive, and she clarified my doubts.

What was your approach to stigmata and bilocation as a nuclear physicist?
I am an engineer, not a physicist; my approach, in this case, was rather emotional, as I saw her suffering with my eyes on Good Friday. I have

always asked doctors and specialists about those episodes. My eleventh book, *Natuzza tra scienza e fede*, is a collection of the opinions of many doctors on stigmata and the hemography phenomenon. Everyone agrees with the fact that these phenomena cannot be explained by science. On bilocation, I will speak later.

Did Natuzza talk to the guardian angels? If so, did you believe her?
The answers given by Natuzza in many situations went far beyond human intelligence. She could deliver very accurate diagnoses, even when the patient was not there, as confirmed by the doctors in my book. I have checked her answers several times to see if she was right. Sometimes, she was too tired to answer my long list of questions, so, before I could ask anything, she provided a single exhaustive response to all the questions I had noted down.

Is there any moment, in particular, that you shared with her and that you will never forget?
Among others, I remember when I witnessed an alleged miracle which, however, I could not document in detail, as I could not contact the participants. I will call it the 'miracle of the deaf and dumb boy.'

One morning, in 1985, I was at Natuzza's house, and I was helping manage the visitor flow. A lady who had not made an appointment came with a child and insisted on seeing Natuzza. The women who were also there to help told her that only the child could be admitted. I noticed that this boy, who was about 10 years old, had a slightly dazed expression on his face.

Natuzza came out the door, pulled the child toward herself, hugged him, and caressed him. I watched the scene and thought: *Now she will heal him with her hands*. She immediately turned to me and gave me a reproachful look, then she took the child with her to the small room where she was receiving. A few minutes later, she came out with the boy and returned him to the ladies who gave him back to his mother, who had remained outside. The next day, his mother came back; she was crying when she knocked on the door and told those women, whom I know personally, that his child had said his first words when he was returned to his mother: "Mom, Natuzza sends you her greetings." That's what I've heard, as I was there.

Unfortunately, I could not contact the child's parents, who were simple and modest people. They came from Puglia. The parish priest's mother saw them enter the church of Paravati and pray in front of the statue of St. Francis and other saints.

We all wondered if this miracle had really happened and I was there when Pasquale, Natuzza's husband, asked his wife, "Natuzza, ask your angel if the miracle has happened and get the names of those people!"

Natuzza immediately replied, "I will never do it. How nice it would be if the Lord performed ten miracles a day, without any of us knowing!"

How do you think the beatification process will end?
I am sure the process will end with her official admission into sainthood, because Natuzza glorified the Lord by loving her neighbor, as He asks us to, and the Lord will sanctify her. It's hard to say when this will happen. For example, the unexpected Coronavirus emergency certainly delayed the process of ascertaining her heroic virtues.

Do you think that the ecclesiastical court will find the "fruits" it is looking for?
The "fruits" are certainly there. She converted half of the population of Calabria, many people in Sicily, Puglia, Tuscany, Sardinia, and beyond. Its cenacles of prayer to the *Immaculate Heart of Mary* are active in Italy, in the United States, in Australia…

How many miraculous events have you cataloged?
There are many "alleged miracles" performed by her when she was alive, while some were reported after her death, but we cannot tell much yet. The Church will investigate and clarify the relevant medical and theological aspects of each single event.

What did Natuzza say about her wounds during Holy Week?
She never called them stigmata, just "wounds". She was a humble woman, and she said that perhaps she was suffering from some disease, to which one day science would give a name. But, of course, she knew very well that they were the signs of her intimate union with Jesus and that she was suffering like Jesus for the salvation of souls.

If Natuzza had lived elsewhere and not in Calabria, would she have become so popular?
I think so, even though she was a typical Southern woman. But she is known all over the world, so… yes.

How much did the press and television contribute to making it an "international case"?
Certainly, the press and especially television have greatly contributed to her popularity. For many, as evidenced by the testimonies, seeing her on TV and hearing her voice was already comforting from a spiritual point of view.

Do you have any unpublished project to be completed on the subject?
I am completing a monograph on the bilocation phenomena experienced by Natuzza, which, as we know, could happen in different ways. Sometimes, when she bilocated, she could be seen in her real body, but she could also be invisible; in this case, she was anticipated by a scent, voices, or noises. She could move objects, carry something from one place to another, leave mysterious blood traces and writings in distant places. This work is an exhaustive study on all these episodes investigated by me. There is also scientific evidence: a blood stain – which was sent to an institute of forensic medicine – was left by Natuzza on a pillowcase during one of these bilocation episodes. The blood type did not belong to the inhabitants of the house, a couple from Catanzaro.

Is there anything, in your opinion, that has been omitted about Natuzza?
Regardless of what was written about Natuzza, this woman will always remain a mystery, because she was so close to and shaped by God that she will never be completely understood, no matter how hard we try. She was also a very discreet person and no one, not even her children or her husband, know all the things that happened to her. Her spirituality could be investigated more in detail, I guess.

A film or a TV show about Natuzza: could it help make this woman an icon?
I think it's too early. Maybe in the future, after her beatification.

Why have you always kept your relationship with Natuzza and Paravati so private, as it was a secret?
I think it's just my nature, and I also believe that each of us has a job to do.
Have you ever been afraid of being "misjudged" by the scientific world for your approach to the case of Natuzza Evolo?

Yes, of course. I have been criticized by some colleagues, but it was not a real problem, as I have always tried to be professional when conducting my studies. For many years, at the end of my Technical Physics course, on the last day of class, I had told my students: 'We have completed the course program; now I will tell you about Natuzza. Of course, you are free to leave if you want to.' But most of them did not leave. And so, for an hour and even more, I shared my experiences with Natuzza with them. Many of these students, several years later, told me that they would always remember that day.

Hearing Valerio Marinelli talking about Natuzza is fascinating; I mean, it's interesting to learn how a professor, a scholar, and a "scientist" approached the case of Natuzza Evolo.

Sergio Zavoli holds her face in his hands, and she reconciles him with God

Sergio Zavoli passed away in August 2020, but there are many memories that bring us back to him and to his special relationship with Calabria, where once he was invited to talk about his professional experience and background to the young people involved in the *Fondazione Natuzza Evolo* project. It was a memorable day. Zavoli arrived in Paravati, which, over the years, had become the real home of Natuzza Evolo, accompanied by the former president of the Regional Council, Agazio Loiero, and the first thing he did upon arrival was to ask to meet Natuzza.

Almost twenty years have passed since that day. It was March 17, 2002, and the meeting organized by the Foundation, with Zavoli and the young people from the Paravati community, was scheduled for 4:30 pm that day. But Zavoli showed up a quarter of an hour late, as perhaps no one had considered the private meeting between Zavoli and Natuzza Evolo. Actually, very few people knew where Zavoli went once he arrived at "Villa della Gioia"; it was him who told the audience about that privileged and special meeting. Zavoli told "his" story to the young people gathered in the room: "Before coming here, I met an extraordinary person with a strong energy; she gave me peace, she brightened up my life, to the point that all my problems seem to be gone. This woman is incredibly humble. I asked her if I could sit down and she replied: 'I am your mother, and you are a son to me'."

Then, he continued: "Today, my journey of faith was made easier. When I saw Natuzza Evolo, in fact, I could feel the presence of God, as it had never happened in so many years of study, research, and conversations with great philosophers and intellectuals of our time.

"It was a memorable day for the foundation," said the current president, Pasquale Anastasi, "as the Foundation had already attended, a short time before, another special meeting between Father Bartolomeo Sorge, a Jesuit from Palermo, and Natuzza, and that Sunday afternoon in March changed the future of the Foundation forever. In the end, both Sergio Zavoli and Father Bartolomeo Sorge had become, without even knowing, the most authentic testimonials of the woman who could 'talk to the dead and to the Virgin Mary', who 'performed miracles', and who, in the Holy Week, lived the great mystery of stigmata."

Before leaving Paravati, Zavoli turned to those young people in the room for the last time to thank them for that special day: "I must confess, I have never seen so many young people attend a conference with such enthusiasm; this proves that something extraordinary is happening here: one soul, many bodies, the same strong faith in God."

When Father Michele Cordiano was asked what Zavoli and Natuzza had said to each other that day, he smiled and tried to avoid answering the question: "When Natuzza met someone, she always closed the door of her room, to keep those meetings confidential. Natuzza never spoke to us about these things. She didn't talk about it with anyone, not even with her husband, Pasquale. Maybe she saw those meetings as a confession, and then secrets she had to keep.

That's what happened with Zavoli. If Zavoli had not told himself that he had met her, no one would have ever known about his conversation with Natuzza Evolo. I can definitely tell that when Zavoli left that room, he was another person. He looked tired and exhausted, even annoyed when he arrived, but after that meeting, he was glowing. It was like he had something to solve when he came, something that he managed to solve when he met Natuzza. I remember he was excited, moved, and amazed by Natuzza."

Before leaving Paravati, Zavoli went back to Natuzza to say goodbye, as he was not sure he would see her again in the future, he held her face in his hands and kissed her on her forehead.

An emblematic image, and a memory immortalized by a photographer who was attending that meeting.

"Natuzza helped me beat cancer", says Ruggero Pegna

In this interview, the popular event promoter from Calabria told what happened the day the doctors told him he only had a few weeks to live, due to severe leukemia. After that day, he visited Natuzza Evolo.

"I had known Natuzza since I was a child, thanks to my father, who was a devotee. Paravati was a sort of Sunday trip for him. We used to enter the hall of her house, on the ground floor – which was crowded – and pray in the chapel. For me, it was a game. She was a reference for my family, a special friend, a supernatural doctor to whom they could ask for advice, especially if someone was ill. So, when I was diagnosed with appendicitis at the age of ten – which required surgery – I asked my parents if we could meet her and ask for a 'miracle'. 'Mrs. Evolo - I told her - I don't want to have this surgery, I'm scared!'. I was also terrified of needles, and surgery was the last thing I wanted to do. She looked at me and tried to convince me that it was something really simple. 'It's like pulling a tooth, don't be scared, it's nothing!' When she saw tears falling from my eyes, she touched my belly and smiled at me: 'Tell the doctor that it was a very bad episode of colitis, you don't need surgery!' That was the moment I thought she was a saint!"

Ruggero Pegna's personal story is strongly linked to Natuzza Evolo. Ruggero is a young Calabrian event promoter who has brought the most popular Italian music artists to the stages of Calabria. Ruggero is a successful man and a promoter of major events, as well as a regular guest of many television programs and important conferences. Yet, despite his success, at some point in his life he had to turn to Natuzza and ask her for help. It must not have been easy for someone like him, who was definitely not a religious person, maybe because he had a rather demanding job, to realize that a poor woman like Natuzza Evolo could, one day, help him heal from an incurable disease.

Ruggero, can we please start from the beginning?
"There are many episodes that link me to Natuzza Evolo and Paravati, in difficult moments of my life, but one is definitely the most noteworthy."

When did it happen?
"It was October 4, 2002. After a summer of intense work, with dozens of events organized, including a show for RAI UNO which took place on September 25 at the Port of Gioia Tauro, I started experiencing sharp pain in the right lower part of my abdomen."

You were supposed to get married the following day, weren't you?
"Yes, I was. It was the day before my wedding. I was worried, so I called my doctor."

How did it end?
"At first my doctors said it was nothing to worry about. Then, when I got a blood count, I was delivered a completely different diagnosis, unfortunately. I was immediately rushed to the hematology ward, at the hospital of Catanzaro, and bone marrow examination confirmed it was acute myeloid leukemia."

What did the doctors tell you?
"It was shocking. According to the head physician, there was no chance I would survive. I was immediately hospitalized to be treated, though."

So, was the marriage canceled or just postponed?

"The marriage was celebrated. My wife wanted to get married as planned. So, instead of the church, we got married in the chapel on the fourth floor of the hospital."

What memories do you have of that day?
"Well, I was really excited, as I was finally marrying the love of my life. However, the worst moments came after that day. Immediately after we got married, I had to start the treatment program designed for all leukemia patients, including chemo, infusions, antibiotics, transfusions, exams, and all sort of therapies. Everything, and even more."

A really shocking diagnosis… have you ever lost faith or hope?
"What can I say? They clearly told me I would not make it. Anyway, from the very first moment – I remember – I began to pray and invoke the presence of Natuzza from my hospital bed. During those terrible days, I had this feeling that Natuzza would help me find the light at the end of the tunnel, which didn't necessarily mean I would recover."

Is it true that she called you?
"No, it isn't. A friend of mine immediately went to see her at her home in Paravati. She told her that I needed to talk to her, that the situation was pretty bad, and that I was hoping to hear from her, and Natuzza replied 'Call him now, and if he can talk, pass me the phone.'"

Do you remember that conversation, Ruggero?
"How could I forget it? 'Do not lose hope' – she told me from the other side of the line – 'the doctors told you what you should expect, but if you fight and accept your suffering, you will win. You'll see.'"

And do you think it was enough to beat cancer?
"No, I don't, absolutely. But that phone call gave me the courage I needed. I found the strength and the hope to deal with that situation. It helped me fight and overcome many difficulties. My God, how many complications! Natuzza even sent me one of her Rosaries, which I always kept in my hands or under my pillow. Now it's on my bedside table, a precious gift!"

What happened after that phone call?

"I had to fight the hardest battle of my life. I underwent my first very intense chemotherapy cycle: ten days during which I have often thought I would not make it. Then, my first progress. The head physician could not believe his eyes: the first cycle did work; may cancer was in remission. Then, I had my second and third rounds of chemo. It was an experience I don't wish on anyone.

"They put me in a sterile room. I remember that I risked dying several times during the treatment due to viral, cardiac, and respiratory complications. One night, my condition got worse. I was very sick. I was wearing an oxygen mask, and, without my knowledge, the doctors had informed my wife, Monica, that my condition was very serious. They were not able to stop an infection that was producing a skin ulcer and injuring my lungs and other organs. One night, as I felt that breathing was getting more and more difficult, I took off my mask, got up, and took the Crucifix from the wall."

Had you lost hope at that point?
"I thought I was going to die, that I was maybe at the end of my journey. I started praying and invoking Natuzza, then suddenly, without even realizing it, I fell asleep. I woke up early in the morning, and I had this strange feeling, as if I had spent the night hugging her and Pope John Paul II."

What happened, then?
"Late in the morning, the doctors came to me, and after another bronchoscopy, they finally identified the virus that was making feel so sick, and I started to feel better."

What about Natuzza?
"After several chemotherapy cycles, I asked to see her in Paravati. It wasn't easy. I could not walk very well and even standing was difficult for me. I depended fully on others."

And what did Natuzza tell you?
"Natuzza smiled at me. She took my hands and said: 'Your Guardian Angel tells me that you are in the hands of excellent doctors. Trust them. I am praying for you, but you have to fight and pray too. Ask for your miracle, and you will get it.' It wasn't enough, though. I remember that I was very

sad and demoralized when I left Natuzza's house. Every single day, during those months, I had this feeling that I was going to die."

Did you go back to the hospital?
"I had to; I had no choice. The hospital had become my real home, treatment after treatment. At some point the doctors told me that I needed a bone marrow transplant, and it was not an easy thing to do."

Did you do it immediately?
"No, I didn't. But the thought of having to undergo a transplant had already shocked me. The idea of a transplant was scary. That's when I decided to talk to Natuzza again. If she had told me that the transplant was not necessary, I would never have done it. I had decided that she was the only person I could trust, regardless of my doctors' opinions."

Ruggero, what did you do at that point? Did you return to Paravati?
"I had to go back to her, to her house. But the day I left to see her, Natuzza was sick. I remember they brought her a note to her room on which I had written questions for her. I needed some answers."

Did Natuzza answer those questions?
"She did, on that day. It was a miracle, believe me. She had dictated her answers to the priest. I read them right away. 'Do what your doctors tell you to do, or you will die.'"

Were you happy with that answer?
"Well, I had no choice. I had to do what she told me to do. I was about to leave, but Natuzza asked the priest who had accompanied me to see me and say hello. They tried to keep her from getting tired, but she was unyielding. I remember that, as soon as I went up to the room she used to receive people who came to Calabria from all over the world, she welcomed me with a hug. It stunned me. She told me: 'The Angel is telling me that you keep calling me. Don't worry, I'm in the hospital with you! But listen to your doctors! Do the transplant. Go to Genoa, they are very good at transplants there!' Her words gave me goose bumps."

Why?
"Because she was right. I was invoking her name every single day."

Did you go to Genoa as suggested by Natuzza?
"I left a few days later. I ended up at San Martino hospital in Genoa, but the doctors told me that the international bone marrow transplant registry had no compatible donors."

What did you do, then?
"I was tired and embittered. I went back to Paravati, to see Natuzza. I felt that I had to inform her of everything, even the most useless detail."

Did you see her?
"Sure. That day Natuzza was particularly sweet, more than she had been in our previous meetings, she smiled at me and said: 'Go back to Genoa immediately. I swear, there is a donor for you… You will see, an American girl will give you her bone marrow. Don't be afraid, do this transplant, and you will finally recover!'"

What did you do at that point?
"The most natural thing in the world. I burst into tears. I did not know what to add or what to say. Before I left, I knelt down, and I remember I kissed her "wounded" hands covered in blood. I thanked her and I cried silently."

And what did she do?
She wanted to hug me, and then she said. 'You have to thank God, not me. This is his plan; I've got nothing to do with it! I'm an uneducated woman, and I'm just repeating what the Angel who is next to you is suggesting. Thank God, Ruggero, and pray!' That's what she said."

Did you go back to Genoa as Natuzza had told you?
"I did, a few days later. I left for Genoa, and, once there, the doctors were informed of the fact that a twenty-four year old American girl had just been added to the registry, and that she could be a compatible donor. And one morning, just out of the blue, this American girl whom Natuzza had told me about months before came to my room."

So, did you do the transplant? How did it go?
"Yes, on July 16, 2003, they took me to the OR for the transplant. A miracle of love that gave me the chance to get back to my life, although there will always be signs on my skin, but I made new friends with whom I shared this journey."

Then what happened?
"Then, I went back to my normal life. I can also tell you that many of the dreams I had at night when I was treated at the hospital really came true. I worked for Elton John and Mark Knopfler, as well as for many other artists."

Is it true that, to thank Natuzza for the amazing gift you had received, you brought music in front of her house?
"It is. When I was discharged, after the transplant, I organized a huge event in her honor, I called it *La Notte degli Angeli*, and it took place in front of the Basilica, a real show with an orchestra and popular artists that could be watched from all over the world thanks to RAI International."

Is it true that, the day Natuzza died you shared a letter with the world through social media?
"Yes, I can read it, if you have time: 'Dear Natuzza, it is hard for me to address you formally. You know, when you've got an angel next you, it becomes a friend, someone you can talk to about everything. Someone who knows everything about you, and who can bring the sun on a cloudy day. Angels are always next to us, they can read our thoughts when we are confused or sad, and they comfort us when we need them. They fly around us. And it's such an amazing feeling that we want them always next to us.

"But angels belong to everyone, so, if someone needs them, they have to go. Knowing you has been a privilege, ever since I was a child. You supported me during my journey, as only angels could do. Now I'm grieving your death, but I know you will be even closer to me. From up there, it will also be easier for you to give a smile to those people from all over the world who need it. Goodbye, Natuzza and thank you for praying for me, for allowing me to kiss your hands, for being an angel in my life. Thank you, for your many miracles of love, including those you made for me."

How do you think the beatification process will end up?
"Honestly, I don't care that much, as Natuzza is already a Saint in my experience. She was a saint when she came to visit me at the hospital, and I felt that she was there. She has never left me alone, and believe me, it is something that I know for sure."

Monsignor Renzo confirms "A new investigation is required. The process of beatification is suspended"

Monsignor Luigi Renzo, Bishop of the Diocese of Mileto-Nicotera-Tropea, the man who, during Natuzza's funeral in Paravati had shouted, "Make her a saint now!" officially said what many already knew, although it was hard to believe.

The Church has temporarily suspended the process of Beatification for the woman from Calabria who could "talk to the dead", and who during Holy Week, "wept tears of blood and lived the great mystery of stigmata." The woman who "talked to Our Lady" and "could bilocate", but who continued to repeat, over and over again, "I am just an earthworm."

The suspension of the Beatification process by the Church was announced with a letter signed directly by Monsignor Luigi Renzo, who also explained why he did not approve of the Foundation that has always borne the name of Natuzza, which, in his opinion, could no longer represent and manage the great media phenomenon of the "Saint from Paravati."

This is the full text of Bishop Luigi Renzo's long letter.

"Dear friends, first of all, I would like to send my regards to all of you, members of the Cenacles of Prayer. I regret to inform you that, in recent days, the Decree approving the Statutes of the Foundation after two years of patient negotiations and ups and downs, was revoked. We are all very sad. However, let me clarify that this order will not affect the Cenacles of Prayer, whose Statutes remain the ones approved in 1999 by my predecessor, Monsignor Cortese. Although they are linked to the Foundation, the Cenacles have been recognized as individual and independent groups by the Church. This means that your meetings can take place regularly, although with the temporary mediation of the Parish of Paravati, as asked by Natuzza. This is clearly written in the Introduction to the articles of the Statutes themselves, whose main paragraphs are the following: 1. 'In recent years I have learned (the words pronounced by Natuzza) that these are the things most appreciated by Our Lord: humility and charity, love and respect for other people, patience, acceptance and the willingness to offer Our Lord what he asks us every day, obedience to the Church'; 2. We shall pray Our Lady with the Holy Rosary, obey the Church, be humble and charitable, and set a good example for other people'; in conclusion: 'The Cenacles want to remain active under the supervision of the Church, like the first Christian community, inspired by the teaching of the Apostles, did ...'

It cannot be otherwise, as the Cenacles and the local Church cannot be separated.

As a Bishop, what I am asking the Foundation is to be the Bishop at the service of this local Church, which needs the Cenacles, as well as other recognized lay organizations. I will strengthen your presence within the Italian dioceses where you are working. With your collaboration, I will also contact the Bishops in the cities where you work, so that your commitment and your efforts can be recognized by the dioceses. This may not be enough, but it is necessary. There could be active Cenacles that are still unknown to local Bishops, and this is not in compliance with the rules of the Church.

The Cenacles are the heart of the Church, and must be recognized and supported by the Diocesan Pastoral Council.

So, there is no reason to worry about what is happening to the Foundation. I am sure that, with the support of Our Lord and Natuzza, everything will be clarified, and we will find a solution. We have already scheduled a meeting with its Board of Directors in the upcoming days, in order to find an agreement that is fair for all the parties. In the meantime, your celebrations at *Villa della Gioia* will continue to take place, and I will participate too, when possible.

I also want to reassure you, because what I am trying to do is not to get rid of the Foundation, or to take possession of its assets, as some have falsely claimed, but only to relaunch the figure and spirituality of Natuzza and her work, which belong to everyone. If this were not the case, it would not even be possible to start the process for her beatification, as we are trying to do.

Therefore, the relationship and collaboration between the Diocese and the Foundation shall be clearly defined from the beginning. Spoken words fly away, written words remain. This is not a personal initiative; I am doing this with the support of the presbyteral council, and, above all, of the Legal Office of the Italian Episcopal Conference, of the Apostolic Nunciature in Italy, of the Apostolic Signatura (the Supreme Court of the universal Church, not a simple Committee, as some have said), and the Secretariat of State of the Holy See.

Finally, I want to reassure you about the consecration of our church, built with your offerings and your sacrifices, for which the Church will be forever grateful. To date, however, being a private church, it cannot be consecrated according to the Code of Canon Law. I will do it as soon as possible, pursuant to article 3 a), the church to be approved, for pastoral care and for worship, is run by the Diocese, as it should be, and a 'Disciplinary Policy' is drawn up before a Notary Public.

I also want to inform you that the process for the beatification of Natuzza has, unfortunately, been temporarily suspended. But, together with the secretariat of the Prefect of the Congregation for the Doctrine of the Faith, we are working to find a way to overcome various obstacles. I am trying to stay positive, and I am kindly asking you to do the same. We must pray, and, above all, make great effort to live as Natuzza taught us, and support each other.

Thank you for what you have done and are doing for our Lord, for the Immaculate Heart of Mary, for Natuzza, and for following her indications: 'Don't look for me, look for Jesus and Our Lady. I am with you and I'll pray for you. The Lord and Our Lady will reward you for what you are doing.'

So, my dear brothers and sisters, I will see you in Paravati for the celebration of August 23. I bless you all, and I ask you to pray with all your heart, so that our Lord and the Immaculate Heart of Mary guide us along the path they built for us."

Therefore, the Bishop confirmed the gathering that is traditionally held on August 23, the day on which Natuzza celebrated her birthday with the cenacles of prayer from all over the world: thousands and thousands of faithful from all over the world, who, every 23 August, return to Calabria, to Paravati to confirm their faith to the "Saint from Paravati."

Natuzza and her intimate relationship with Jesus

Il Gesù di Natuzza is the latest book by Luciano Regolo, Deputy Editorial Director of *Famiglia Cristiana*, which has been recently published by Edizioni San Paolo. This book investigates the relationship between the mystic from Paravati and Jesus.

The preface is written by Don Antonio Rizzolo, head director of *Famiglia Cristiana*, while the author is Luciano Regolo, a charismatic journalist from Calabria, who was born in 1966. Today, he is the Deputy Editorial Director of *Famiglia Cristiana*, but he has been an influential columnist and a news correspondent for major national newspapers.

He wrote several books on the subject for Mondadori, including *Natuzza Evolo. Il miracolo di una vita* (2010), *Natuzza amica mia* (2011), *Il dolore si fa gioia: Padre Pio e Natuzza. Due vite, un messaggio* (2013), *Le lacrime della Vergine* (2014), and *Dove la Madonna parlò a Natuzza* (2014). He is clearly an intellectual who knows much more about Natuzza Evolo than anyone else. He had access to some confidential and private documents, which, today, are being examined by the Vatican as part of the beatification process.

"Ten years after her death," writes Luciano Regolo in his essay, "we can say that Natuzza Evolo's personal story was the story of mystical conversations with saints, with the Virgin Mary and with Jesus, which have marked her entire life and were collected in some books describing a woman who was very simple and could interpret the Gospel and the Core message of Christianity."

In fact, this book contains a sort of a "Christology according to Natuzza", as reconstructed by Deputy Editorial Director of *Famiglia Cristiana*, to confirm that the message from the mystic from Paravati is consistent with the evangelistic message. But also to point out that the idea that Natuzza had of Jesus was quite innovative, as she felt she was, at the same time, her daughter, and her mother.

"In fact, Natuzza loved Jesus as a mother loves her son, nothing more," points out Luciano Regolo, "a new perspective, then, offered by Natuzza Evolo, who can be considered, therefore, as one of the great interpreters of Christian theology."

"What was absolutely impressive," writes Don Antonio Rizzolo, head director of *Famiglia Cristian,* in his preface, "is her ability to handle those extraordinary phenomena she had experienced throughout her life. This is why I put aside my prejudice, as sometimes those who have such special gifts lose sight of the essential aspect of those events, that is, spirituality."

The head director of *Famiglia Cristiana* has no doubts about the "Case of Natuzza Evolo", as it can be deduced from what he says about the new essay by Luciano Regolo: "When reading this book, Paul's letter to the Galatians – which Giacomo Alberione, the founder of the Society of St. Paul, to which I belong, loved so much – came to mind several times: *I have been crucified with Christ; and no longer do I live, but Christ lives in me; and the life which I now live in the flesh I live in the faith of the Son of God, who loved me, and gave himself for me. […] I bear the marks of Jesus in my body.*

"They sound like the words Natuzza might have said, although, when St. Paul, mentioned the 'marks', he probably meant the sufferings of his apostolic ministry, and not the fact that he had real wounds on his body."

His words are pretty clear, but Don Antonio Rizzolo goes even further: "Based on the same reasoning, the reference to the crucifixion suggests an association with the phenomena experienced by Natuzza around Easter. What St. Paul is saying is that, after realizing how much Jesus loves him, his life has changed. That's why he says *and no longer do I live, but Christ lives in me*. This is the essence of every authentic Christian life, the key point of every true mystical experience. This book is entirely focused on the intimate relationship between Natuzza and Jesus, and this love is the key to understanding the meaning of a life completely devoted to the Father."

We all knew that Natuzza had a connection with the afterlife, as this is what they have been telling us for half a century. But today, an authoritative and charismatic intellectual of the Church like Don Antonio Rizzolo finally helps us better understand the long journey taken by Luciano Regolo to investigate the life of the mystic from Calabria: "Her conversations with the Lord were more like dialogues between lovers, which confirms that they had a really intimate relationship, and that there was a close bond between them."

In this regard, the book includes a message left by Padre Pio to Natuzza in 2020, during Lent, which gives a clear idea of her love for Jesus: "God's love cannot be compared to earthly things [...]. The most beautiful day is the day you choose God as your friend. This is the greatest love of all [...]. What is God? God is joy, love, mercy, and peace. Who can feel God's presence? Those who listens to the voice of God inside them. I have experienced God's love and now I know what it is. It's holy love, pure love, the one that makes you feel on top of the world." This intimate relationship between Jesus and Natuzza is not over, and is not exclusive open to others. In 2001, for example, Jesus said to the mystic: 'Romantic love is not the only type of love. You can find love everywhere in the world.' This is the type of love that there should be between every Christian and the Lord."

Wonderful. But there's more.

According to the head director of *Famiglia Cristiana,* "This principle recurs several times in the messages that Natuzza received from Jesus, and, above all, she put those messages into practice by helping other people, even if sometimes all she did was give advice and smile. I have said a lot, but I invite you to read *Il Gesù di Natuzza*.

Let me just add something. The most important thing that makes this woman a saint is her humility. Humility is the foundation of all the other virtues. Well, Natuzza's humility is, in my opinion, the most amazing quality of this woman. Not only did she define herself as an 'earthworm', she even tried to hide, to minimize those gifts she had received. And this made her suffer, although she always tried to stay positive. The book, among other things, contains an episode that reveals this aspect. One day Don Pasquale Barone, the parish priest, told her that he wanted to introduce her to a very popular friar, but Natuzza replied: 'I don't want to meet important people! I just want to meet those in need'."

"Why the rush to make Natuzza a saint? Her miracles? Many cases of alleged healings."

Don Enzo Gabrieli, born in 1972, earned a bachelor's degree in theology from the *Seminario Regionale San Pio X* and a Licentiate in Sacred Theology from the Pontifical Gregorian University. Today, he is considered one of the most interesting intellectuals of the Church in Calabria. A philosopher, but also an experienced and prolific journalist, Don Enzo was ordained a priest during the Great Jubilee in 2000, and after working as a secretary for the Archbishop of the Diocese of Cosenza-Bisignano, he became parish priest of the Parish of San Nicola di Bari in Mendicino, a small town of 10,000 near Cosenza.

As the AGESCI (Association of Italian Catholic Guides and Scouts) ecclesiastical assistant, he has mainly dealt with social communication for many years. He manages the office of Church-related social communications of the Archdiocese of Cosenza, but above all, he has been the head director of *Parola di Vita* – a weekly magazine about the most salient facts of one of the most influential and most innovative dioceses of the Church in Calabria. As a theologian, he knows much about "saints", and was called by the Church of Rome to deal with some of the most important canonizations for the Archdiocese of Cosenza, including the ones involving Venerable Elena Aiello, Gioacchino da Fiore, and Elisa Miceli.

Today, Don Enzo is, above all, the Postulator for the Beatification process of Natuzza Evolo. Not an easy task, which has turned him, despite his discretion, into one of the points of reference for the case of Natuzza Evolo. Don Enzo agreed- for the first time – to talk about the process initiated by the Vatican for the Beatification of the mystic from Paravati.

How far has the process for the Beatification of Natuzza got? When do you think the process will be concluded? In other words, how long do we have to wait? Years?

They have been collecting information about Natuzza for years, and some witnesses have already been called to attest to the candidate's goodness.

Does this mean that we have to wait for years?
Well, what is called the 'informative process' is quite long. It's a very delicate stage, as all data and testimonies are being collected to confirm Natuzza's devotion to God and other virtues. So, not 'sainthood now', as Cardinal Amato said, but 'sainthood for sure'. This is how the diocesan tribunal and postulation work. Many documents are being collected and this is good.

Is it true that you have been working hard, struggling with all those documents to be analyzed?
Absolutely, yes. But, in my opinion, it's not done yet. We will have to work for a few more years, which is hard but also rewarding, because listening to all those amazing stories that seem to be written by God himself is an incredible experience. You can get confirmation of the existence of God, and your faith is strengthened every time you discover a new, incredible story about Natuzza.

Don Enzo, can you tell us if the Congregation is investigating some episodes that could be considered "miracles"?
There are many reported cases of alleged healings. There are also many alleged miracles. That's why we are asking for more documents. People who shared those stories with us believe that God worked through Natuzza's intercession, but for the process to come to fruition, those testimonies must be supported by accurate documentation.

What do you mean?
Well, many miracles are "graces" instead, which are also important, but are also very difficult to prove according to the procedures. However, they can help assess her lifestyle, her reputation, and even her virtues, as she was a servant of God who has comforted and supported many people who have knocked on the door of her house - and of her heart, of course.

When dealing with causes of beatification, we often hear about the "fruits of holiness"; in this case, are there any "fruits" that could help to successfully complete the beatification process?

The fruits are those we are collecting from the testimonies. Many people have returned to God, they have changed their lives, they have been reconciled with God and with other people. They have also returned to the Catholic Church, which was critical. During these years, hundreds of prayer groups have been started – the so-called cenacles – and many people have tried and still try to follow her example, to make small and big sacrifices, to accept pain and suffering as part of life. Others try to emulate Natuzza and her trusting obedience to the Church. I believe these are all signs of true devotion, and whoever does this wants to walk her path to holiness.

I guess it's not an easy job for you, is it?
Well, all these phenomena can be disorienting. But the Church guides us, helps us to purify false devotion. For example, I think that Natuzza wanted us each to be more humble. In fact, she described herself as an earthworm, a woman deeply in love with Christ and the Church. She continued to obey the Church, even in the most difficult moments, and she has never lost hope.

Can I ask you what is your personal opinion on the case of Natuzza Evolo? Do you believe what has been said for years?
A Postulator is never impartial or completely neutral. When you meet a saint, you are bewitched by him or her; you can smell their scent, see their beauty, and even their souls. I do not want to disclose the opinion of the Church's on Natuzza or on the phenomena experienced by her. However, I can say that Natuzza has lived a simple life, which is exactly what the Gospel says. She was a mother to many people who were suffering in many different ways. She shared the gifts that she had received from God with other people; she opened her heart. In my humble opinion, the most impressive thing about her was not her mystical experiences, but her love for the Church, and the support she offered to many people while she continued to take care of her family.

Did you focus specifically on the wounds and the blood experienced by Natuzza during Holy Week?
All the documents we needed have been collected. Many of them are quite accurate, while others are just opinions. But medical and theological experts will give their final opinion on these phenomena.

Will their opinion affect the cause?

Wounds and blood, but also other phenomena on which the Church is investigating and will investigate, do not tell you much about her holiness. These phenomena concern her, only her, as it happened with Padre Pio, Beata Elena Aiello, and other saints. What happened to them was due to her special charism, and to their participation in the passion of Christ.

What does all this mean?
It means that her virtues tell more about her holiness than all those episodes do. I mean, her faith, her hope, her love for God and for other people, and then her patience, humility, fortitude, poverty... as far as we know, Natuzza has never asked for money, nor has she ever rebelled against the Church. She just accepted sufferings and difficult challenges. She even ended up in a mental institution.

Can I ask what do you think about the very complex phenomenon of bilocation and the visions that Natuzza claimed to have of heaven or hell?
These phenomena, witnessed by some, are also being studied. We can't say anything about it yet. What I can say is that these bilocation phenomena have been experienced by other saints, and therefore they are possible.

Do you mean previous similar episodes?
Yes, of course. Padre Pio, for example, or San Pietro d'Alcantara, Sant'Alfonso Maria de' Liguori, San Clemente Papa, St. Anthony of Padua, St. Francis of Assisi, San Francesco Saverio, San Giuseppe da Copertino... There are other examples like these, such as San Martino de Porres, San Filippo Neri, San Giovan Giuseppe della Croce, San Giovanni Bosco, but also San Francesco di Paola. And, about the visions of heaven or hell, we had Fatima, Santa Teresa d'Avila, Santa Veronica Giuliani, Saint Faustina Kowalska.

And, what about the angel Natuzza claimed she was talking to?
Talking about these phenomena requires knowledge and extensive research. At the same time, they must be contextualized. Cultural and mental categories also alter how these episodes are described. Angels can be sent by God. The Bible is full of visions of Angels. The Virgin Mary and Saint Joseph spoke with Gabriel the Archangel, for example. And after them,

other saints talked to or were guided by angels. Some saints claimed that they saw the guardian angels of other people.

I remember another mystic from Germany whose name was Mechthild Thaller von Schönwerth (1868-1919). She was from Munich, and she could talk to the Angels and said that she had seen the guardian angel of some saints. This conversation could go on and on... The Seers of Fatima, for example, were prepared for First Communion by an angel who introduced itself as the Angel of Portugal. St. Thérèse of Lisieux also cherished a special devotion to the Holy Angels, and explained how to have a direct relationship with them, how to invoke them, and be guided and guarded by them.

Are there any cases examined by the Church that are similar to the case of Natuzza Evolo?
Well, something very similar happened with Edvige Carboni from Sardinia. She was born in 1880 in Pozzomaggiore and died in Rome in 1952. She also had the same gifts and similar visions. Elena Aiello is more popular in Calabria, as she was from Cosenza.

Can I ask you if the negative opinion given by Father Agostino Gemelli could slow down or negatively affect the process?
Father Gemelli was an eminent scholar and his doubts, as well as his research, may support the investigation that the Church will conduct. He also raised doubts about Padre Pio, but as a doctor, his scientific position did nothing but clarify some aspects. Science can really help in these cases, and should not be considered as an obstacle.

In fact, when it came to deciding whether some episodes were "miracles", scientists simply said they could not be explained from a scientific point of view. When they are asked to give an opinion, theologians start from this assumption and then decide if certain episodes can be considered "miracles", which are more about faith and intercession. They are two different points of views, and they should not be confused.

Father Agostino Gemelli was a man of faith and a researcher, and *Cattolica University* and Fondazione Policlinico Universitario Agostino Gemelli in Rome are its legacy to the scientific world. He also made his personal contribution to the Church, to society, but when these two dimensions overlap, for example in the case of Padre Pio, he made some mistakes. For example, he wanted to analyze the phenomena of Sister Elena Aiello, but he was not authorized by the Congregation for the Doctrine of the Faith (formerly the Holy Office). Perhaps that was due to his personal approach to these phenomena.

It seems that it will take some time for the Church to finally conclude the process, doesn't it?

Now, it's time to pray, to contribute with testimonies and writings, to find the truth about this wonderful figure of our time. We have to wait, patiently, and we must also trust the Church, which knows how to deal with these events. Hopefully, Natuzza Evolo will soon be proclaimed a saint. What we can do is imitate her virtues, her lifestyle. We don't have to look for Natuzza or invoke her; we have to look for Jesus and the Virgin Mary, and love the Church, with its strengths and weaknesses.

Every day, a thousand fresh flowers on Natuzza's grave

Today Natuzza Evolo rests here, in her private chapel, in her old birthplace. On her headstone, we find her name, her date of birth, and the day of her death. There is also a big photograph, where she looks beautiful and serene, as she was when she was not sick, and found her inner peace.

Thousands of people stop here, in front of her tomb, every day.
These people come from all over Italy and Europe. A week after her death, her people gathered again, and will continue to gather here, where the church that Natuzza had strongly wanted is about to rise.

The prayer march in her memory starts at 9:00 in the morning, and goes on for hours. First, there is the procession of the statue of the Virgin Mary, which is carried on the shoulders of believers throughout the town, then the solemn homily of the bishop, Don Luigi Renzo. In the front row, Natuzza's children and grandchildren watch intently.

Natuzza is already a saint to Don Luigi, and she must be celebrated as such. It is no coincidence that this young and extraordinary intellectual from Calabria compared the dust storm that accompanied the death of Jesus at Golgotha to the storm that accompanied the death of Natuzza in Paravati.

Everyone is free to believe, but this huge crowd of people gives us an idea of the legacy left by Natuzza on earth.

Don Luigi Renzo closes his homily with a long letter that the cardinal, Monsignor Tarcisio Bertone, sent to the community gathered for Natuzza, to thank the Lord for this extraordinary gift of love whose name was Natuzza.

The rest is history, but here, in Paravati, eleven years after Natuzza's death, nothing has changed, and the great woman, a mystery of faith, has not yet been revealed.

Don Attilio Nostro: "Natuzza, prophecy and fulfilment"

Like in the past. Thousands of people gathered, on November 1, 2021 – twelve years after her death – in the churchyard in Paravati, where Natuzza had the Great Basilica built, so that her devote followers could pray at her tomb.

During the solemn homily celebrated by the new bishop of Mileto, Monsignor Attilio Nostro, who succeeded Monsignor Luigi Renzo – Pope Francis' special messenger in Calabria, indeed – Natuzza Evolo's Sanctuary was mentioned, which has not yet been opened for worship. Hopefully, according to Don Attilio, this could finally happen.

"Pray," said Don Attilio Nostro, "not just for me, but also for this amazing work (clearly referring to the Basilica), which is another milestone achieved by Natuzza. Pray until this church is finally consecrated. (At that point, the audience unanimously rose to its feet in a standing ovation). Pray that I may continue what was undertaken and started by Monsignor Oliva, thanks to this invaluable agreement, also strongly desired by the Pope. I spoke to Monsignor Oliva last night, and he asked me to send you his greetings. And may this be a sign of reconciliation!".

But the young bishop said much more.

"The Foundation and I want the same thing: that all the misunderstandings and difficulties – sometimes even incomprehensible – that you have encountered, or should I say, that we have encountered in recent years may now belong to the past. Pray that the peace of God may rule in my heart, and in the hearts of those who will work with me to make this happen. Pray that this sanctuary may become what it was and is in the heart of God. A place where souls can take refuge. A place where murderers can be reconciled to God, repent, mend their ways, confess. A place where offenders can realize that there is an alternative to crime. A place where husbands and wives can reconcile. A place where kids can fight for a new world. A world where even priests can rediscover the glory of the priesthood, that love and faith that made them give up everything and follow God".

"I hope – continues the bishop, speaking off the cuff – "that walking through that door, that door that leads to God's mercy, and once out, people can finally say 'God spoke to my heart'".

This time, the Pope has really hit the mark.

After reflecting on, and discussing it for weeks, which is absolutely normal in these cases, the Church has finally chosen the new bishop of the Diocese of Mileto-Nicotera-Tropea. One of the most illuminated and best prepared priests in Rome: Don Attilio Nostro, who was born in Palmi, but actually raised in Rome, where he studied, lived and breathed the Gospel, first, and then Doctrine and Liturgy, when the young priest joined the Pontifical Lateran University. Here Don Attilio studied, and here he became one of the most interesting philosophers of the Church of Francis.

His first meeting with the faithful, in one of the 'busiest, most difficult, and even most discussed' places in the history of the Calabrian church will go down in history.

"Pray for me. I have just become the bishop of this diocese, and I don't know you well yet. Pray for me, pray that God may enlighten me. So that my choices are always guided by brotherhood and by the mercy of God. And God is not a judge, He is a father. But, there will come a day when we will all be judged by Him".

In the large clearing in Paravati where the Basilica strongly desired by Natuzza Evolo – and expressly requested by the Virgin Mary, who appeared to Natuzza, as told by the mystic from Paravati during one of her interviews – was built years ago, just a stone's throw from her birthplace, the new bishop confessed that he had contacted Natuzza in the past and that he had come to visit her in her home.

"Today is the first of many other days, which sees me as a pilgrim, a beggar, a doubtful and even pretentious man. During two other meetings I had with Natuzza, I told her how difficult it was to be a priest. I never imagined that I would become her bishop. So, having the opportunity, today, to repay the love with which this servant of God welcomed me with all this love means a lot to me. I hope to live up to her concern and to the fraternal charity she showed me, as a man and, above all, as a Christian minister."
Don Attilio talked about Natuzza for sixteen minutes, confidently and without interruption.

"We are gathered here today to celebrate the solemnity of all Saints, and to recall that day when she left this earth to go to Heaven, although she actually became united with God when she was baptized. And this is an opportunity for all of us to renew our faith and our baptism, as we are all here – like many years ago – to find the answers to our questions. Questions, sometimes even terrifying, that we carry in our hearts and that we no longer want to ask".

"Sometimes, we doubt God, when our religious faith is shaken by illness and disability. And we feel betrayed by God after a loved one dies. We think that God, our Father, let us down. That God was distracted. We think that God does not treat all of us equally".

"That's why Natuzza is a sign on this Earth. Natuzza is proof that God is not distracted, that He has a plan for all of us. And all of us who have met her, who have had the opportunity to see her and hear her, have been impressed by her concern. Her message could be summed up in a few sentences: 'You are not alone'. 'God is walking beside you'. 'God knows you'. 'God does not make mistakes'. We are the ones who made a mistake when we doubted God, indeed".

Don Attilio's final warning to the people gathered to celebrate Natuzza is even more solemn.

"At the end of your day, do not settle for the many things they have told you, the things you have heard, the things they offered to you. Read the Holy Scripture. Even in the morning, before starting your day. What the Church asks us to do as deacons, priests and bishops is beautiful. It asks us to open our lips and mouth to proclaim His praise. Knowing that the Cross of Christ is the first to touch your lips in the morning, when we wake up, is a beautiful thought. Waking up with the taste of this kiss on our lips, the kiss that God gives us when we touch the Cross of Christ. Isn't it beautiful? Starting and ending our day with prayer. This is what matters, because it means that God is in the center of our life. It means absorbing God's Word. It means that we are not alone when we suffer, when we struggle".

And, getting back to Natuzza.

"And how can a reconciled heart not accept that mysterious story, that unforgivable past? How can we love others if our heart does not know peace, forgiveness and mercy? That's why, faced with our helplessness, we have to get down on our knees, join our hands, and pray. And Natuzza showed us the way. We are not just a number. We are here to make the difference. We are here to ask God: 'Come and fill my heart, as it is empty without You! Fill my heart, or it will be filled with a thousand useless spirits. Grace me with Your presence, Lord. Grant me the faith I need tomorrow'. And so, with this beautiful page from the Gospel, the Lord tells us that we are all Blessed".

The audience responded with thunderous applause. Like in the past, when thousands of people used to gather in front of Natuzza's house, waiting for her to show up and give them a sign. As if she were still among us. The new bishop? There couldn't be a better choice! Don Attilio' spoke to Natuzza's people from the heart, and these people could see it and welcomed him with open arms. And chose to love him.

The new bishop was also warmly welcomed by Pasquale Anastasi, President of the Immaculate Heart of Mary, Refuge of Souls Foundation (Fondazione Cuore Immacolato Di Maria Rifugio Delle Anime).

"His words confirm, once again, the support offered by the Church to our current and future projects. We left the past behind, we are on the same page now, and we would like to work with the Church to complete the project that the Virgin Mary asked Natuzza to implement as early as 1944. I am here to assure you, Your Excellency, and to confirm, if necessary, that our Foundation is willing to walk alongside, and work with the Church, as the Church recognized Natuzza's testimony of faith".

"The Basilica will be finally consecrated in August 2022"

Don Attilio Nostro, the new bishop of the Diocese of Mileto-Nicotera-Tropea, announced that the Great Basilica in Paravati, which is the church that Natuzza Evolo had built before her death, will finally be opened for worship and officially consecrated. That's really good news!

"See you on August 6, 2022, the Feast of the Transfiguration, for the consecration of this beautiful church!"

This is the solemn and official announcement made by Monsignor Attilio Nostro, the new bishop of the Diocese of Mileto-Nicotera-Tropea, at the end of the Eucharistic celebration presided over by him, on March 5, 2022 at 4.00 pm in the Cathedral-Basilica of Mileto.

"Allow me to thank – continues Don Attilio Nostro – all those who, in a number of ways, have assisted, supported and encouraged me with their prayers during this period: first of all, the priests of this amazing Diocese of

Mileto-Nicotera-Tropea, especially Don Pasquale Barone and Don Michele Cordiano; and then, the Immaculate Heart of Mary, Refuge of Souls Foundation… last but not least, thanks to all of you, brothers and sisters, who have never stopped praying for this blessed day to come! I really appreciated it, as faith and the power of prayer move mountains! And the grace of God will give us strength and help us become more of what we already are: beloved children of a wonderful Father who loves us immensely, of a crazy and beautiful love! Pray for me!".

"Today, – adds the bishop – a prayer of praise to God resounds over this square, to celebrate the union of the Immaculate Heart of Mary, Refuge of Souls Foundation and the Diocese of Mileto-Nicotera-Tropea. After having traveled together a path of knowledge and mutual esteem, we have finally come to the decision to consecrate and open this church for worship and prayer".

"We want a heartfelt appeal – concludes the young bishop – to follow Jesus Christ and become, like Him, the Light of the world, resounds throughout this church! Fortunata Evolo, our beloved 'Servant of God' saw herself as a simple messenger referring the faithful to the Virgin Mary and Christ! Why should we come on pilgrimage to Paravati? What gift will God give us by consecrating this church? The gift offered by this pilgrimage will be the LIGHT of the Transfiguration of Jesus, which illuminates the darkness of the world and of men! 'You shall be holy, for I, the Lord your God, am holy'. 'I Am the Light of the World. Whoever Follows Me Will Never Walk In Darkness, But Will Have the Light of Life'. Thus, those who come out of this place will bring the Light of Christ to the world!".

The audience applauded Pope Francis' messenger, perhaps sent to Calabria for a specific reason: restarting dialogue between the official Church and Natuzza's devote followers delivering them the most solemn and most important message that the Vatican could send to Calabria.

Natuzza Evolo: her first official biography by ICSAIC

In Calabria, Mother's Day coincided for at least twenty years with a major event in Paravati, during which thousands of mothers from all over Italy came to see Natuzza Evolo up close "to ask her for a favor". ICSAIC, the Calabrian Institute for the History of the Anti-Fascism and of Contemporary Italy, managed by Pantaleone Sergi, a journalist and a former la Repubblica correspondent, published, in June 2021, the first official biography of the "woman who talked to the dead and who lived the mystery of blood and the stigmata." The author is journalist Pino Nano, and the biography is available at. http://www.icsaicstoria.it/evolo-natuzza/.

notes

notes

Pino Nano Copyright-2022

Made in United States
North Haven, CT
19 July 2023